GRACE THAT
OVERCOMES

Life Transforming Devotions

Bishop Darlingston G. Johnson, D.Min.

www.xulonpress.com

Table of Contents

Introduction

To understand the grace of God is to understand the love of God. He blesses our lives for our good and His glory. Acts 20:32 says, *"So now, brethren, I commend you to God and to the word of His grace, which is able to build you up and give you an inheritance among all those who are sanctified."*

God's plan is to build you up. He has an inheritance for you. This is what God has determined for His children. Yet, too often, those who love Him do not understand how to apply the word of grace so that their lives manifest God's best. We can learn how the word of grace builds us up and begin to experience our glorious inheritance right here, right now, regardless of our circumstances.

Grace works in your life. This devotional tells you how.

Be blessed,

Bishop Darlingston Johnson

Day 1

The Greatest Welcome Ever!

U nder the Old Testament, entering the presence of God was a very risky and fearful thing. When God gave The Ten Commandments at Mount Sinai, He established physical boundaries to prevent the people from coming too close to Him lest they die. Only the High Priest, once a year, had His permission to enter the Holy of Holies, but only after engaging in an elaborate rite of purification. Anyone else who came into the Holy of Holies perished!

Because of the holiness of God and the sinfulness of man, it was as though a huge warning sign had been erected in the Old Testament around God for all people to see, which said:

"Warning: This is a no sin zone. No sinners allowed. Unless you are perfect, you are not welcome here. Stand back."

But all of this changed when Jesus died for the sins of the world and offered His blood to the Most Holy God for our sins. God accepted His sacrifice as full payment for every sin of every person for all time, once for all. The Bible declares,

> *"For by one offering He has perfected for-*
> *ever those who are being sanctified."*
> (Hebrews 10:14)

Jesus' sacrifice of His own body on the cross for the sins of the whole world accomplished what the blood of a million bulls and goats did not do. It satisfied God's holiness and justice perfectly. It took sin out of the way completely. It obtained eternal redemption. It perfected sinners and made them as pure in the eyes of God as the blood that purified them!

Now, because of Jesus, God has taken the warning sign down! And replaced it with a new sign – a huge welcome sign erected around Him for all to see. It reads something like this:

"Welcome: This is a grace zone. All sinners allowed. If you have ever sinned, you are welcome here. Draw near!"

> *"Therefore let us draw near with confidence*
> *to the throne of grace, so that we may receive*
> *mercy and find grace to help in time of need."*
> (Hebrews 4:16, NASB)

The blood of Jesus dealt so effectively with our sins that God no longer needs to separate Himself from us. So instead of warning us to keep our distance because of our sins, lest we die, He now commands us to draw near to Him, so that we may live. And whereas in the Old Testament, only the high priest could enter the Holy of Holies once a year, because of Jesus, God has chosen today to make His home in us!

Child of God, believer in Jesus, this is good news. If you are in Jesus, not even your sins can separate you from God because He has promised, *"I will be merciful to their unrighteousness and their sins and their lawless deeds I will remember no more"* (Hebrews 8:12). Nothing shall be able to separate you from God any more.

So, today, when you have a need, remember you are forever forgiven and forever welcome to draw near to God to find grace and obtain mercy. And remember, because of the effectiveness of the blood in taking away all our sins once for all, you will always meet a smiling Father saying, "Welcome, how may I help you?"

And that's the greatest welcome ever!

Affirm Today:

"I draw near. I am forgiven and clean. My life is different and I live in this world as Your heir, set apart for Your glory."

Additional Scriptures:

Hebrews 4:16; Hebrews, 10:14; Hebrews 8:12; Hebrews 8:10; Ephesians 1:7

Day 2

Let God Pay the Bill

L et me show you how to frustrate the grace of God in your life. How to stop His unmerited, unearned, and undeserved favor and blessings from flowing freely in your life. How to make Jesus' death of no benefit to you. If you desire this for yourself, or for anybody you know, then look at Galatians 2:21, for the way to do so.

> *"I do not frustrate the grace of God: for if righteousness come by the law, then Christ is dead in vain."* (Galatians 2:21, KJV)

There it is. All you have to do to frustrate the grace of God, stop the flow of blessings, and make the death of Christ of no benefit to you is to believe that your righteousness comes by the law. Just start thinking and acting like you must merit righteousness, just insist on trying to qualify for God's favor by your adherence to His laws, and you will nullify the grace of God in your life. You can either be blessed through the law, or by grace, but never through both (Romans 11:6).

What is grace? It's unmerited, undeserved, unearned favor. It is God choosing to bless you based solely on His love for you. It is God qualifying you for every blessing based on the death, burial, and resurrection of Jesus. It is God not requiring you to give Him any reason to bless you other than Jesus' sacrifice. It is God paying the bill in full.

Suppose you take a friend out to dinner as a way of showing him you love and appreciate him. You have a nice dinner and good time together, but when the waiter brings the bill, your friend grabs it. You request the bill, but he refuses to give it to you. You insist that he lets you pay for the meal because he's your guest and you want to do this as a gesture of your love. But he adamantly refuses to give you the bill. No," he says. "I'm going to pay." Finally, frustrated by his insistence, you let him have his way.

And so, he writes the check for the bill. Unfortunately, when it is presented to the bank, the check bounces. Insufficient funds! How sad – because of pride, your friend not only frustrated your grace, he embarrassed himself! It would have been so much better if he had just received your kindness humbly and let you pay the bill.

God the Father has paid the bill. He plans for you to enjoy all of His blessings without any charge to you. So don't try to earn His favor and merit His blessings, because sooner or later, you will discover your "funds" are insufficient. Don't frustrate God and embarrass yourself by being self-righteous. On your best day, you sin and fall short of His glory.

"I do not frustrate the grace of God," Paul wrote. "If God wants to bless me without requiring me to give Him a reason to do so, let Him. If He wants to forgive me of all my sins, declare me one-hundred percent righteous, meet every need I have, and shower me with His love and kindness, without regard to my performance under the law, I will not get in His way. I accept His grace gladly."

Child of God, don't grab the bill and frustrate His efforts to bless you. Your "funds" are insufficient anyway. Your "self-righteousness" is as filthy rags. Just be grateful for His love for you and Jesus' sacrifice on your behalf. And then respond in childlike trust, with worship, and thanksgiving, and love.

Affirm Today:

"I am blessed because God loves me and I am qualified for every blessing based on the death, burial, and resurrection of Jesus."

Additional Scriptures:

Galatians 2:21; Romans 11:6; Acts 20:32; Romans 3:24; Psalm 84:11

Day 3

Rest and Receive God's Best

A re you "standing on the promises" of God as you await a breakthrough? That's what I used to do. But as it is with standing physically, I discovered the manner in which I was "standing" on the promises could be exhausting. Standing for long periods of time wears you out! But I've found a better way.

Instead of standing on the promises, I have learned it's much easier and far more effective to rest in them. And in fact that is what God wants us to do. I found that "standing" on the promises tends to keep the focus on me, but "resting" in them keeps the focus on the One who matters, Jesus!

> *"There remains therefore a rest for the people of God. For he who has entered His rest has himself also ceased from his works as God did from His. Let us therefore be diligent to enter that rest, lest anyone fall according to the same example of disobedience."* (Hebrews 4:9-11)

In the passage above, God invites us to be diligent to enter His rest. That is, hasten to do so. Why? Because that's what it takes to enjoy Him fully. When we rest, we receive God's best! "I can't afford to rest," you say. "There's just too much to do. Too many devils to fight. Too many temptations to resist. Too much to accomplish for Jesus." You're right, there's too much to do. That's why you need to rest. You see, when you rest, God works. And He actually works through you!

What are we to rest from? Rest from depending on our own works and self-efforts to be righteous in God's sight and accepted by Him. Rest from trying to be good enough to earn His favor. Rest from trying to impress Him with our religious activities. We are to cease from our own works!

Now, do not misunderstand. The rest God is speaking about is not to stay in bed all day, refusing to have a job, being irresponsible. The rest spoken of is the rest that occurs when you take your eyes off of yourself altogether and stop trying to merit God's blessings. It is the rest you experience when you believe He Himself is doing His work in you and through you. It is a rest given to you, even while you are doing all you should be doing. It is the rest of faith.

You see, there's only one thing God requires of us. And that is for us to hasten to enter His rest. It is for us to be quick to take our eyes off ourselves. Be quick to cast our burdens upon Him. Be quick to come to the throne of grace and mercy and cast the responsibility of all our cares upon Him and refuse to pick them up again. All He requires is for us to rest confidently in His finished work and then boldly confess our faith in who He is, what He's already done, and what He's doing now.

Child of God, instead of trying to earn salvation and blessings, learn to rest in the promises of God, already finished and completed by Christ. Learn to rest in His gift of righteousness and stop trying to establish your own. Learn to rest in His gift of love and power, not only to save you, but to keep you. Instead of trying to live victoriously in your own strength, realize your victory does not depend on how strong you are, but how strong Jesus is. Instead of trying to be good enough, realize God blesses you not because you are good, but because He is.

When you rest, you enjoy God's best!

Affirm Today:

"I rest in Your gift of righteousness, love, and power. You are keeping me and I am blessed because You are good."

Additional Scriptures:

2 Corinthians 1:20; Deuteronomy 28:6; Matthew 6:31-32; 2 Chronicles 15:4; Hebrews 4:9-11

Day 4

Small Change, Big Difference!

Israel had two opportunities to enter the Promised Land – first under Moses, and forty years later, under Joshua. The first time they failed to enter; the second time they succeeded. What changed? Not God and not His purpose for them. God never changes, and His purpose for His people is forever established. Not the Canaanites. They were still far more numerous and stronger than Israel. If neither God, nor the Canaanites changed, what did? Israel's attitude! Israel's faith!

The first time they received the opportunity to enter into Canaan and take possession of their inheritance, their attitude doomed them. They said, "The Canaanites are too strong for us, we are too small for them, and we are not able to enter." The second time, however, their attitude was different. "The Canaanites are too strong for us, we are too small for them, and we are not able to enter. But we will trust God, nevertheless, and still enter, because even though we are not able, we know for sure our God is able to take us in." A small change, it seems, but what a big difference it made in the outcome!

What caused the change in Israel? Forty years in the wilderness. The "wilderness" is a place of no resources, where you cannot help yourself or solve your own problems; where you must learn to depend completely on God's grace and mercy to survive. It is intended to reveal to you that you cannot save yourself, that you have no strength to meet your own needs, and your success and your very survival depends completely on your willingness to look to God's grace and mercy alone.

What a valuable lesson for you to learn today! Your Promised Land is Jesus Christ and all the good things that are already provided for you in Him. Like Israel, you are not able to take possession of His fullness and abide in Him in your own strength. The world, the flesh, and the devil are far too strong for you. But like Israel, God wants you to go ahead, and without looking at yourself, take possession of His fullness by faith, anyhow. Your attitude should be, "But I will trust God, nevertheless, and still enter, because even though I am not able, I know for sure my God is able to take me in."

Child of God, do you need a change in your attitude? Do you know that taking possession of your inheritance, enjoying the fullness of Jesus Christ, does not depend upon your strengths? Have your wilderness experiences taught you yet that your supposed strengths won't qualify you, and your many weaknesses won't disqualify you? That God Himself will take you in, even though you are very weak? Israel learned this lesson in the wilderness, and it changed their experiences completely.

This is good news, indeed! In spite of all the things in your life that make you unable to enter into your promised land, because of Jesus you can still enter. And, child of God, when you choose to enter His fullness by faith in His finished work, His fullness will enter your experiences. Small change. Big difference. Wow!

21

Affirm Today:

"I confidently walk in victory. I know You have planned good things for my life and I rejoice in my destiny. My future is secure. Jesus, I am forever grateful. "

Additional Scriptures:

Joshua 1:8; Exodus 14:14; Deuteronomy 31:6; Philippians 4:13; Joshua 1:16

Day 5

The Father's Wish

I have a question for you. Can you tell me the number one reason Jesus died for you? My answer to that question used to be, "He died to forgive my sins so that I could go to heaven to be with God when I die." I believed this until the Holy Spirit opened my eyes and showed me I was wrong.

The day Adam sinned, he died spiritually. That is, his sin separated God from him and erected a barrier that remained in place for thousands of years between God and man. Man was put out of the Garden and cherubim placed at the entrance to ensure he did not re-enter. And later, during the Old Testament dispensation, God commanded Moses to place a thick veil in the tabernacle that would maintain this separation between God and man due to sin's presence in man.

To help ameliorate the crisis caused by sin and the resulting separation, God instituted a temporary priesthood in the Old Testament that offered animal blood to atone for man's sins. This system allowed for limited interaction between God and sinners, but never resolved the core issue of sin and spiritual death. It allowed for sins to be covered, but never removed. Consequently, the veil remained in place, the people served God at a distance, and only the High Priest could go beyond the veil into the Holy of Holies once a year. Even then, he had to observe very strict rules, or else!

And so we read in Hebrews 10:4-7 and 10:

> *"For it is not possible that the blood of bulls and goats could take away sins. Therefore, when He came into the world, He said: "Sacrifice and offering You did not desire, but a body You have prepared for Me. In burnt offerings and sacrifices for sin You had no pleasure. Then I said, 'Behold, I have come— In the volume of the book it is written of Me— To do Your will, O God'...and by that will we have been sanctified through the offering of the body of Jesus Christ once for all."*

It is written that God took no pleasure in animal sacrifices. His heart remained heavy. Why? Even though millions of bulls and goats were sacrificed, the sin issue remained unresolved and the wall of separation remained in place. God, who is love, could not be pleased as long as our sins were separating Him from us.

Jesus saw the broken heart of His Father, a loving Father who wanted intimacy and constant fellowship with the only ones He had created in His image, a Father who wanted men to experience His love personally and intensely. Seeing that His Father's heart was unhappy, and that the longing of the Father was to dwell with us and make His home in us, Jesus, whose love for the Father is immeasurable, requested that a body be prepared for Him. He was going to do whatever it took to do the Father's will and bring pleasure to His Father's heart.

And so Jesus received a body, went to the cross, became sin, was separated from God, descended into hell, suffered the full punishment for sins; and on the third day, He arose, ascended into heaven, and with His own blood sanctified us once for all!

The day He shed His blood for sinners, the veil of the temple split in two. The barrier that existed between God and sinful man came down. For the first time, since Adam sinned, God was free to make His home in us. The Father's wish was finally realized.

This is what the Holy Spirit showed me! The number one reason Jesus died for me was not to make it possible for me to go to heaven to live with God when I die, but even better, to make it possible for God to dwell in me while I live! As much as Jesus loves me, I now see it was God's desire to dwell in me and Jesus' love for the Father that motivated Jesus the most to offer Himself to reconcile God and me.

Child of God, the longing of the Father has always been to dwell in us, to be our Father, Provider, Protector, and Friend. Thanks to Jesus, whose blood cleanses us from all sins, the Father's wish has been accomplished. Today, God is pleased because our sins can no longer prevent Him from living in us and fellowshipping with us.

Because of this blessed reality, if your trust is in the blood of Jesus, you can enjoy uninterrupted intimacy with God. Nothing, I mean absolutely nothing, can separate you from His love. Not even your sins!

Affirm Today:

"I joyfully accept what Jesus did for me. Father, my life is wonderful because You live in me. I am always with You, blessed and reassured. I now allow myself to walk in this reality every day."

Additional Scriptures:

2 Timothy 1:9; Ephesians 1:4-6; Psalm 18:35-36; Colossians 1:27; Hebrews 10:4-7, 10

Day 6

The Real Reason Jesus Died for You

I used to believe that the primary purpose for Jesus coming to die for sinners was to qualify them to go to heaven to be with God when they die. Now, this is one of the many blessings we receive through our faith in Christ. And I look forward to experiencing heaven when I die!

But I've recently come to see something about Jesus' earthly mission that heretofore I had not seen so clearly. Contrary to what most Christians believe, qualifying sinners to live in heaven was not the major reason Jesus came to earth. This may surprise you, but this is true.

Hebrews 10 tells us God was not pleased with the sacrifices of bulls and goats. And why? Because those sacrifices did not solve the problem of separation between the Most Holy God and sinful man, whom He loved so perfectly. And this was painful to a loving, Heavenly Father who longed to live within His people!

> *"For the law, having a shadow of the good*
> *things to come, and not the very image of the*
> *things, can never with these same sacrifices,*
> *which they offer continually year by year,*

27

*make those who approach perfect. For then
would they not have ceased to be offered? For
the worshipers, once purified, would have had
no more consciousness of sins. But in those
sacrifices there is a reminder of sins every
year. For it is not possible that the blood
of bulls and goats could take away sins."*
(Hebrews 10:1-4)

Consequently, Jesus obtained a body prepared for Him,
and came on a special mission of love. It was to do what the
blood of bulls and goats failed to do. Jesus came to do the
Father's will. He would offer a sacrifice capable of making
the worshippers perfect and pure, having no consciousness of
sins. He came to reconcile God and sinners by taking away
sin once for all. (Hebrews 10:5). And He did.

On Friday, while still hanging on the cross He shouted,
"It is finished." Then on Sunday, when God raised Him up,
God shouted, "Amen!" Sin, the thing that had required God
to separate Himself from us, had been dealt with perfectly,
once for all. The veil of the temple, which symbolized the
period of separation between God and man was taken down,
and that sad period came to an end.

*"For by one offering He has perfected for all
time those who are sanctified."* (Hebrews
10:14, NASB)

Having sanctified and perfected believers for all time,
Jesus accomplished the will of the Father finally. He successfully removed the sin barrier that kept God from fulfilling the
longing of his heart – to love and live in us! He presented God
with the greatest gift He could give His Father, the one thing
God did not have, a sacred home within the hearts of men.

Now, because of Jesus' finished work, Paul could write to believers, saying,

> *"Don't you realize that your body is the temple [the very sanctuary] of the Holy Spirit, who lives in you and was given to you by God? You do not belong to yourself, for God bought you with a high price. So you must honor God with your body."* (1 Corinthians 6:19-20, NLT)

Today, I realize the number one reason Jesus went to the cross was not to meet our needs, but to meet His Father's need. It was not because our sins kept us from God, but because our sins kept Him from us. His greatest motivation was to meet the desire of His loving Father to love and live in us.

Child of God, while it is wonderful that you will go to heaven when you die, what is even more wonderful is that Jesus has qualified you to be the very sanctuary of God on earth. Heaven has come to you!

Now, live like it is so!

Affirm Today:

I am excited and expectant because I am prepared for heaven and for earth. I am perfect before God. My life is set apart for every good work."

Additional Scriptures:

Hebrews 10:1-4; Hebrews 10:5; Hebrews 10:14; 1 Corinthians 6:19-20; John 3:16

Day 7

Are You a Victim of Identity Theft?

Identity theft is a huge problem in the U.S. Every year billions of dollars are stolen by people pretending to be someone else. I was a victim myself last year. And because my identity had been tampered with by some unscrupulous person, my credit card was blocked and I was unable to transact legitimate personal business. It is extremely important to protect your identity from thieves.

What is true of your physical identity is even more true of your spiritual identity. If Satan is permitted to tamper with your revelation of who you are in Christ so that you are confused about how God sees you and whom He has made you to be, he can wreak havoc and make your life miserable and unproductive. And you will find yourself struggling to transact legitimate spiritual business on behalf of yourself and others. Things that should be easy, like releasing faith for miracles, receiving answers to prayers, overcoming temptations, leading sinners to Christ and ministering to others will become nearly impossible.

That is why in writing to saints who were experiencing fiery trials, Peter reminded them of whom they were with these words:

"But ye are a chosen generation, a royal priesthood, an holy nation, a peculiar people; that ye should shew forth the praises of him who hath called you out of darkness into his marvelous light: Which in time past were not a people, but are now the people of God: which had not obtained mercy, but now have obtained mercy." (1 Peter 2:9-10, KJV)

Note these facts about your spiritual identity, God's child:

You are chosen. You did not beg God to accept you. You did not have to. It was He who pursued you. It was He who asked you to accept Him. He loves you.

You are royal. You do not need to be impressed by British royalty. Why? You are royalty yourself. You are a member of the family of God, a born-again child of the King who created, owns, and runs the universe. Royal blood flows through your spiritual veins and arteries.

You are holy. That which is holy is set apart unto God to be used for uncommon purposes. Your faith in Jesus has set you apart for God's glory. You have ceased to be common. You are no longer ordinary. You are clean.

You are peculiar. Not odd, but special. In a peculiar way, unlike other people, you belong to God. His own, special possession!

You are a priest. That's right, an "ordained" one too (John 15:16, KJV)! You do not need to confess your sins to any man to be forgiven by God; you do not need to experience God through anybody. You have direct access to God yourself. And you are privileged to be a full time minister with the power to bring God and men together in Christ Jesus.

You have obtained mercy. You will not experience the judgment you deserve. Instead of punishing you for your sins, God has forgiven you of all of them and decided to shower you with unmerited favor and blessing through Jesus. You are a vessel of mercy and not of wrath.

Child of God, this is awesome. Protect this revelation. Refuse to permit the thief to tamper with it. It is most valuable to you as you conduct personal spiritual transactions. Never forget, this is who you are in Jesus!

Affirm Today:

"I celebrate my identity in You. I am chosen and I am royal. I enthusiastically embrace this truth. My life is a life of power because I am part of Your holy nation."

Additional Scriptures:

1 Peter 2:9-10; John 15:16; Deuteronomy 7:6; Ephesians 1:13; Romans 3:24

Day 8

Have You Made Christ of No Effect to You?

I t is sad, but true, that you can make Christ of no effect to you. That is what Galatians 5:4 states: *"Christ is become of no effect unto you, whosoever of you are justified by the law; ye are fallen from grace"* (Galatians 5:4, KJV). And when that happens, you cut yourself off from God's unmerited favor and blessings. Now, can you really afford to let that happen?

Yet, it happens far too often. Like the Galatians, believers have a tendency to forget that they cannot justify themselves by law-keeping. They try to deserve the Father's blessings through their hard work. To merit His answers to their prayers by their commitment to Him and their service. They inwardly hope He is impressed with them enough to give them more "grace."

But such an attitude towards God achieves the exact opposite. It ties God's hands and renders His grace ineffectual in our lives. And the reason is simple. When we are depending upon ourselves for justification, or for favor with God, we are not looking to Christ. We are not drawing on His Life, making a demand on His ability, or releasing our faith in His power. We have essentially, often unintentionally, turned our

backs on Him and all He offers in order to secure our blessings through self-effort. We have made Him of no effect.

What I am describing is similar to what would happen if
a person switches off the light in a room at night. By choice,
he makes the electricity available in the room of no effect to
him. And as a result, he is immediately plunged into darkness.
Now, in order to see, he tries to find a match, but he has none;
and so he stumbles in the dark.

Is this happening to you? Are you stumbling in the dark
because you have made Christ of no effect in your daily
life? And have you made Christ of no effect by unbelief and
self-effort? If so, stop right where you are today, and get back
into the flow of God's grace and love. "Flip the switch" to
"on" again.

Child of God, Jesus is everything God needs from you,
and everything you need from God. So, take your eyes off
of yourself and fasten them on Him. Agree with the Father
that you will not ever try to deserve His favors again. Instead,
every day, and in every situation, you will always look to
Jesus for the life you need from Him to live the life He wants
from you. By so doing, you will become established in the
grace of God, the work of Christ will take effect in you, and
you will start to partake of the power of Christ daily.

Now, that's something you cannot afford not to let happen.

Affirm Today:

"I release myself from my ability and welcome God's ability
in my life. I now allow myself to relax. Father, I lovingly
trust Your grace and awesome love for me. I look to You for
the life I need from You to live the life You want from me."

Additional Scriptures:

Galatians 5:4; Psalm 18:30; Acts 1:8; Mark 1:17; John 15:5

Day 9

Reprogram Your Mind

"If any man is in Christ he is a new creature." God fundamentally changes a person when he or she receives Christ as Savior. He regenerates them spiritually, imparting to them His very own nature. This is the experience Jesus referred to as being "born-again" in His conversation with Nicodemus in John 3.

If you are a born-again Christian, this has happened to you. You are not the same person spiritually you were before you accepted Christ. You are a forgiven person. God has removed all your sins, past, present, and future, off of you. And He will never charge you with sin again as long as you are in His Son. He has also made you totally brand new!

We could say, God has replaced your hardware completely. The old equipment crashed. You could never live the life God planned for you with the old spirit you came into this world with. It was irreparable. So He made you a completely new spirit. A spirit-person made in the image of His Son (Colossians 3:10)!

Now, your new "hardware" requires new "software" to run the program God designed it for. You have the right hardware to bear the fruit of the spirit, to manifest God's power and display His glory in a manner that others can see. But like a computer, your new spiritual hardware requires the right software, the right information, to operate effectively.

God is always ready to reveal this information to you in His Word and by His Spirit. But it's your responsibility to download this information, divine revelation, into your heart and mind. You do so by spending time with Jesus in prayer and by meditating on the Word of His grace, the finished works of Christ, the promises of God, and other new covenant blessings. You do so with the goal of renewing your mind and reprogramming the way you think about God and about yourself.

Here is what Paul had to say about this.

> *"I beseech you therefore, brethren, by the mercies of God, that you present your bodies a living sacrifice, holy, acceptable to God, which is your reasonable service. And do not be conformed to this world, but be transformed by the renewing of your mind, that you may prove what is that good and acceptable and perfect will of God."* (Romans 12:12)

Child of God, God has graciously provided you with the hardware you need for victory. All you need now is the right software. And that is available to you too, just waiting to be downloaded into your heart and mind. So what's stopping you? Begin the download now. Begin experiencing victory today. Begin living the Christ-life today. Reprogram your mind!

Affirm Today:

"I let go of old ways of thinking and doing and welcome my new mind transformed by God's Word."

Additional Scriptures:

2 Corinthians 5:17; John 3:3; Colossians 3:10; Romans 12:1-2; Ephesians 1:3.

Day 10

Receive Blessings, No Curses

W hat do you think of this statement, "Do good, God's glad. Do bad, God's mad"? If you believe this is a true statement and it is consistent with the New Testament, you are wrong. The truth is, God's opinion of us in the New Covenant is not based on our performance, but on Jesus' performance. So He does not get mad with us when we do badly. We are His beloved and He is pleased because we are in Jesus.

In fact, because of Jesus, God's not even mad at sinners anymore! And because of His substitutionary death on the cross for all sinners, God is no longer imputing their trespasses to them.

> *"And all of this is a gift from God, who brought us back to himself through Christ. And God has given us this task of reconciling people to him. "For God was in Christ, reconciling the world to himself, no longer counting people's sins against them. And he gave us this wonderful message of reconciliation." (2 Corinthians 5:18-19, NLT)*

A wonderful message, indeed! Because of His great love for us, God sent Jesus once for all, *"to put away sin by the sacrifice of Himself."* (Hebrews. 9:26). As far as God is concerned, Jesus has solved the sin problem completely, something the blood of animals never did. And when He considers the sacrificial blood His Son was willing to shed on behalf of sinners, God is glad, not mad.

It is true that in the Old Testament we see the wrath of God being poured out upon sinners. But that was because the Old Covenant was based upon the law of sin and death. Under the New, however, we learn that *"Christ has redeemed us from the curse of the law by becoming a curse for us in order that the blessing of Abraham might come upon the Gentiles"* (Galatians 3:13-14). And that *"the law of the Spirit of life in Christ Jesus has set us free from the law of sin and death"* (Romans 8:2).

What we need to really understand, brethren, is that the New Covenant the Father made with the Son on our behalf is not a continuation of the Old Covenant. It is not a modified version, or an improved version. It is completely new and completely different. It is based on grace, and not law. And unlike the Old, it contains only blessings and no curses for all those who have placed their faith in Jesus.

Does this mean I am now going to live in sin because I know Jesus has redeemed me from every curse and God does not get mad with me or withdraw from me when I sin? Of course not! Why not? Firstly, because I don't want to. Secondly, because sin is poison. If I drink poison, it will do me much harm, not because God is mad, but because poison is bad. Sin is bad. Like poison, it kills!

Receive God's love, enjoy unmerited favor, be forgiveness-conscious, and tell others the good news of a God who is reconciled to them and is reaching out to them to be reconciled to Him. Tell them the good news of the Son who died for them!

Affirm Today:

"I am rejoicing and walking in my New Covenant relationship. I am dazzled by Your love and I am free. Your favor and blessings overtake my life and victory is mine."

Additional Scriptures:

2 Corinthians 5:18-19; Hebrews 9:26; Galatians 3:13-14; Romans 8:2; Galatians 5:1

Day 11

The Sin Solution

W ant to know the solution to sin – to the penalty, power, and presence of sin? It's not The Ten Commandments. It is not the fear of judgment. It is the revelation of Christ. It is GRACE!

> *"And of His fullness we have all received, and grace for grace. For the law was given through Moses, but grace and truth came through Jesus Christ."* (John 1:16-17)

Moses brought the Law and, with it, the threat of curses for breaking it. But sin continued to reign. The fear of judgment did not stop sin.

Then Jesus came bringing grace and truth – that is, the truth of salvation by grace through faith in Him – and the religious leaders killed him. The message of grace, instead of law, scared them.

What is it about grace that scares folks? I've actually been cautioned by ministers that "even though we know that we are totally forgiven of all our sins, past, present and future, through Jesus, we must be careful how we preach this to the immature Christians because they will use that knowledge to sin."

Brethren, if we don't preach the grace of God only, what are we to preach? Law? A mixture? No wonder the body of Christ is in such bad shape. How sad!

Grace is not a doctrine; it is a person.

Grace is Jesus in all His fullness and in all His works.

To distrust grace, therefore, is to distrust Jesus and His finished work. To think that preaching pure grace leads to sin is to believe that preaching only Christ crucified, apart from law, results in sin. How can that be? Are we not complete in Christ? Is faith in Jesus not enough? Must we add our works to His to be secure in Him?

Instead of giving people permission to sin, the revelation of God's grace accomplishes just the opposite. It is the sin solution!

> *"For the grace of God has appeared that offers salvation to all people. It teaches us to say "No" to ungodliness and worldly passions, and to live self-controlled, upright and godly lives in this present age."* (Titus 2:11-12, NIV)

There is only one antidote to sin, and it is not The Ten Commandments. It is pure, unadulterated grace made available through the Gospel to all who hear and believe.

Preach the law to people in order to make them live holy lives and you will strengthen the power of sin in their flesh. It will be impossible for them to overcome.

> *"The sting of death is sin, and the strength of sin is the law. But thanks be to God, who gives us the victory through our Lord Jesus Christ."* (1 Corinthians 15:56-57)

Preach only the Lord Jesus Christ, the Grace of God, to them and He will give them the victory.

Romans 6:14 reads:

> *"For sin shall not be master over you, for you are not under law, but under grace."*

> *"For if by the one man's offense death reigned through the one, much more those who receive abundance of grace and of the gift of righteousness will reign in life through the One, Jesus Christ."* (Romans 5:17)

Hallelujah! Listen to what the Apostle is saying. Don't throw the law at sin – that's like adding gasoline to fire. Don't use guilt and condemnation to try to get people to stand up and walk straight. That won't work. Throw grace at sin, and not just a little amount. Let grace super abound.

Men will succeed in overcoming sin under grace, who fail under law. Why? Because the man who is under law is trying to work for God, but the man who is under grace has God working for him!

Child of God, grace, not law, is the sin solution.

Affirm Today:

"I live by grace and not by law. Because of Jesus I am forever free."

Additional Scriptures:

Titus 2:11-12; 1 Corinthians 15:56-57; Romans 6:14; John 1:16-17; Romans 5:17

Day 12

True Love

I drew a line in the sand. "Enough is enough. Today, you have to choose between me and him." And so at the ripe old age of fifteen I already felt I was entitled to the exclusive affection of the girl I was "in love" with. I would not tolerate any competition. Forced to choose, she did. Unfortunately, she did not have enough sense to choose me. She chose George! I went home and went to bed, a rejected boy. So if you think I am messed up today and in need of serious counseling, that's why. Blame this girl who did not have enough sense to know what was good for her!

But thank God, one person's trash is someone else's treasure. While others may reject you, God does not. When He had to decide what to do with you, He chose you.

> *"You have not chosen me,"* Jesus said to His raggedy bunch of disciples, *"but I have chosen you and ordained you to bear much fruit and that your fruit should remain."* (John 15:16)

And just look at these powerful words penned by the Apostle Paul in Ephesians 1:3-5:

"Blessed be the God and Father of our Lord Jesus Christ, who has blessed us with every spiritual blessing in heavenly places in Christ, just as He chose us in Him before the foundation of the world, that we should be holy and without blame before Him in love, having predestined us to the adoption as sons by Jesus Christ to Himself, according to the good pleasure of His will."

Now, those verses actually say that God chose you before He started to create the world! That suggests He created the world for you, and He created it with you on His mind!

I was meditating upon this truth some time ago when I sensed God saying something like this to me: "Son, I created the world for you, not for me. And you, I created for Myself, not for the world."

Wow, I am God's true love! Chosen, loved, and accepted in Christ Jesus – if that can't undo the damage done to my self-image by that girl who had no sense but to choose George over me, nothing else can!

Beloved, you can't make everybody accept you, or love you. It would be nice were that the case, but it just isn't going to happen. But should that really be a big deal since according to the Scriptures, you are God's true love?

This fact alone, that God loves you and has created you for Himself, should make you want to hug yourself and say aloud, "I am, of all men, most blessed."

So go ahead and do it! You have a right to feel very special. After all, the King of kings has chosen you for Himself.

Affirm Today:

"I am God's true love! Chosen, loved, and accepted in Christ Jesus. I am blessed and highly favored."

Additional Scriptures:

John 15:16; Ephesians 1:3-5; Ephesians 1:6; Galatians 3:26; Romans 8:38-39

Day 13

Does Life Have You All Locked Up?

Thank God for principles and propositions. They have their place. But when you are really locked up by trouble, it's not what you know, but whom you know that really matters.

Paul understood this well. Old, cold, and locked up in a Roman dungeon for the sake of Christ, he encourages his spiritual son, Timothy, with these words:

> *"For this reason I also suffer these things; nevertheless I am not ashamed, for I know whom I have believed and am persuaded that He is able to keep what I have committed to Him until that Day."* (2 Timothy 1:12)

At a time when life looked dreary, with hands and feet chained, sitting in a dark, damp prison, Paul found strength, not in what he knew, but in Whom he knew. He boasted not in his great knowledge of principles and propositions, but in his intimate knowledge of a Divine Person – his Lord Jesus Christ!

"There are many things I am uncertain of right now," Paul would say. "I don't know all that might happen to me as a result of this imprisonment. But there is one thing of which I am absolutely confident, and this brings me great comfort, I know Whom I have believed and am fully convinced that He is watching over and caring for me."

Child of God, don't be satisfied until you too can say this with confidence. Don't be satisfied with just knowing principles and propositions. Make it your goal, and pray to grow in your revelation of Jesus Himself, to see Him in the Word and in your experiences. Then, during those times when trouble surrounds you, you will not be afraid. You will find great strength and comfort in the One you know, the Man, Christ Jesus.

You see, ultimately, it's not what you know, but Whom you know that really matters.

Affirm Today:

"For I know Whom I have believed and am persuaded that He is able to keep what I have committed to Him until that Day. Locked doors are open and I am free."

Additional Scriptures:

2 Timothy 1:12; John 4:42; Ephesians 3:17-19; 1 Corinthians 1:9; 1 John 1:3

If You Only Knew How Powerful You Are!

Do you live as an eagle or a chicken? A lion or a mouse? A king or a slave? Ephesians 1:16-23 paints a breathtaking story for us of what God accomplished through Jesus' death and resurrection and Paul's prayer is that our understanding will be flooded with light so that we can truly see how exceptionally powerful we are in Christ Jesus. One of the things he prays for in verse 19 is that every child of God would know the power of God that is "to us-ward who believe." That is, that each of us would know the amount of power that is available to us for carrying out God's will for our lives; the amount of power that is in us to work for us and through us in every situation we face in life; and the amount of power that is available to us at all times to live truly successful and victorious lives.

Paul describes the power for us the best he can but he declares that really it is past human understanding. That is, language is inadequate to describe it. He uses a Greek word that can be translated "surpassing greatness, vast, unlimited and immeasurable." The power available to us who believe is so vast that it is inadequate just to call it great. It is immeasurable – you cannot quantify it. It is unlimited—it has no ending or maximum point to it. It can never run out or be exhausted.

Paul says, this is the same "mighty power" God exerted to raise Jesus from the dead when all of hell tried to keep Him in the grave – it is therefore resurrection power; to lift Jesus up to heaven when all of hell tried to keep Him under – it is therefore ascension power; to exalt Him far above principalities and powers and every name that is named in heaven and on earth when all of hell tried to keep Him in subjection – it is therefore dominion power. Paul's prayer is that all believers in Christ would know that God has placed resurrection power, ascension power, and dominion power in them and that this power is available to them all the time to accomplish His purpose for their lives.

Furthermore, according to Ephesians 1:22-23, God has put all things "under His feet" and made Him the Head of the Body, which is the Church. Note, all things are placed not just under the Head of Jesus, but under the feet of Jesus too. Now, the last time I checked the feet were part of my body and in the lowest position physically. So, if you are a part of Jesus' body, even if you think you occupy the lowest position in that body, all things are in subjection to you in Christ!

You say, if this is so, how come I am living such a powerless, ineffectual and defeated life? Listen to me, an army of sheep led by a lion will defeat an army of lions led by a sheep any time and any day. Why? Because if lions think and act like sheep, no matter how loud their inherent roar might be, and how strong their jaws and muscles, they will respond to their enemies like sheep and run in fear rather than stand and rule. The problem is, if a king thinks and acts like a mere slave, then even a powerless enemy can make him afraid and cause him to fall apart mentally, emotionally, and spiritually. And as long as believers continue to see themselves as nothing more than guilty sinners, or at the very most, forgiven sinners, they will always operate in powerlessness and a defeated devil will still triumph over them.

So what is the answer? Believers need to know by revelation who they are and what they have in Christ Jesus! They need to see that the Son of God became the Son of man so that the sons of men can become the Sons of God. Their hearts and minds need to be flooded with the revelation that they are now the Sons of God, invested with the power of God and the full authority of Jesus Christ to use His immeasurable power to enforce His will on this earth.

What should you do? I suggest you take the prayer recorded for us in Ephesians 1:16-23, and begin praying it for yourself and other believers daily. And meditate continually on the Gospel, which is the message of God's unconditional love and grace, received by faith in the finished work of Christ. As you pray and meditate consistently on the message of grace, the Holy Spirit will open your eyes and you will come to know progressively and personally that power which surpasses human understanding.

This power is to those who believe. To believe practically is to live in accordance with. So stop arguing with God's Word, stop disqualifying yourself, and start living in accordance with this truth – your spirit is enthroned with Christ and you are wearing the garments of spiritual royalty.

If you only knew how powerful you are, your days of walking in fear and defeat would be over!

Affirm Today:

"I am sealed by Your Holy Spirit. My inheritance is guaranteed. I now relinquish fear and defeat and welcome power and victory. I joyfully receive the spirit of wisdom and revelation in the knowledge of Jesus. And daily I am learning the hope of my calling in Christ."

Additional Scriptures:

Ephesians 1:16-23; Ephesians 1:22-23; Ephesians 1:15-23; Psalm 94:14; Joshua 1:9

Day 15

Stop Calling Yourself a Sinner

D o you refer to yourself as just "an old sinner saved by grace?" If so, you should stop it. Why? Because it is not the truth! And you are contradicting Scripture and weakening yourself spiritually by doing so. You see, you can be "an old sinner," or you can be "saved by grace," but it is not possible for you to be both at the same time.

Once you received the grace of God and experienced salvation, you ceased being an old sinner. You became a born-again child of God, a new creation, the righteousness of God!

> *"Therefore, from now on, we regard no one according to the flesh. Even though we have known Christ according to the flesh, yet now we know Him thus no longer. Therefore, if anyone is in Christ, he is a new creation; old things have passed away; behold, all things have become new."* (2 Corinthians 5:15-17)

> *"For He made Him who knew no sin to be sin for us, that we might become the righteousness of God in Him."* (2 Corinthians 5:21)

This passage instructs you to stop defining yourself by what you look like outwardly and start seeing yourself as you are in Christ Jesus – new, clean, forgiven, and righteous.

"But," you say, "Even though I know I am saved by grace, I know also I do still sin. Doesn't that make me an old sinner saved by grace?" No, it doesn't. It makes you a saint who has some growing up to do. It makes you a child of God who still needs to discover how much God loves you and the exceeding great power that works in you. (See Ephesians 1:15-19).

You need to see that salvation changes your nature completely. It is similar to what happens to a caterpillar when it changes into a butterfly. Once the caterpillar goes through metamorphosis and is "born-again," it ceases to be what it was and becomes something totally new. It ceases to be an earth-bound creature crawling in the dirt, and becomes a butterfly, equipped with wings, flying up above.

Now, who refers to a butterfly as a "caterpillar that flies?" Nobody in their right mind! It used to be a caterpillar, but it is definitely not a caterpillar any longer. People see it as it now is; not as it was at one time.

Does a butterfly occasionally land on things below and get dirt on its wings? Yes, but will that cause it to become a caterpillar again? No, once a butterfly, always a butterfly!

Child of God, how you see yourself is critical to your growth spiritually. If you continue to see yourself as "an old sinner," you are going to continue to behave like an old sinner. And that's just what the devil wants. But if you allow the Spirit of God to renew your mind with His Word so that you see yourself as the righteousness of God, always holy and blameless in His sight, not because of what you do, but because of Whom you have inside of you, sin will no longer reign over you. Instead of struggling to do works of righteousness, and failing, you will begin to produce righteous deeds effortlessly as the fruit of your new nature.

Affirm Today:

"Christ has set me free and I am holy and blameless, a saint of God. I embrace my new life and my new nature. I make righteous decisions and empowering choices that reflect who I am now."

Additional Scriptures:

2 Corinthians 5:21; Ephesians 1:15-19; Romans 12:1-2; 1 John 3:7; Matthew 6:13

Day 16

Discovering Prayer

felt it – a dull, aching, ever-present pain. I touched it – a growth on my body. It scared me. I was only fifteen. Weeks passed. No change. Desperate, I went into my parents' bedroom. Alone and frightened, I prayed. "Jesus, please heal me. Please, Jesus, heal me. Please!"

Then it happened. Instantly. Suddenly. It felt like Someone had touched the spot where the growth was. Startled, I reached for the area. It was gone. It had vanished. The growth had disappeared instantly. It never returned. My prayer was answered.

So how potent is prayer? Very! It activates the miracle-working, dead-raising, need-supplying, demon-destroying power of God to accomplish the will of God on earth. How important is prayer? Extremely! It actualizes and personalizes the blessings of redemption. "You have not because you ask not." So says the Apostle James.

Prayer is essential. Praying occupied the Lord Jesus during His earthly life. He lived to pray. In fact, He still does.

> *"But He, because He continues forever, has*
> *an unchangeable priesthood. Therefore He*

*is able also to save to the uttermost those
who come to God through him, seeing he
always lives to make intercession for them."*
(Hebrews 7:24-25)

Observe what occupies Jesus right now in heaven. *"He
always lives to make intercession."* This means, at this
moment in Heaven, He is literally giving His life over to this
great ministry of intercession for us. He is praying for us.
Jesus is our heavenly Intercessor.

Now, if He is giving His life to interceding for us in
heaven, then this ministry of prayer must be very precious
to Him. It must also be very important to the Father, since
Jesus does only what is pleasing to the Father. And it must
be absolutely essential to the New Covenant!

Indeed, it is. It was essential for Jesus to die on the cross
for guilty sinners to provide redemption. But in order to make
His sacrifice effectual, in order for us to reap the benefits of
His death, He had to appear in Heaven before the throne of
the Father and intercede for us on the basis of His death. Had
Jesus not followed up His sacrificial death with His interces-
sory life, no one would have reaped any benefits from His
death. Oh, how very important prayer is!

Child of God, prayer makes personal and experiential
what redemption made legal and real. It actualizes what the
Cross potentialized. Without it, the blessings of redemption
will elude us. We reap the benefits of Jesus' death and take
possession of our inheritance by prayer based on the finished
work of the Cross!

Listen to Jesus' words on this. *"Then He spoke a parable
to them that men always ought to pray and not lose heart"*
(Luke 18:1). Child of God, discover prayer. Take possession.
Learn to pray.

Affirm Today:

"I am reaping the benefits of Jesus' death and take possession of my inheritance by prayer based on the finished work of the cross."

Additional Scriptures:

Hebrews 7:24-25; Luke 18:1; Luke 11:2-4; Proverbs 15:29; James 5:16

Day 17

So, You Think God Can't Use You?

I remember playing sports and choosing teams as a young man. The best players were always chosen first. You chose the best players in order to gain the advantage over the other team and hopefully ensure victory for your side. But God is not like that. When God chooses, He does not look at what we have, but at what we don't have. He chooses those who are needy and who have nothing to offer Him except weakness and foolishness. He picks those the world would disqualify and makes them His co-laborers; members of His team.

1 Corinthians 1:26-28 teaches that God "chose" the foolish, the weak, and the despised. That is, He did not end up with these people because He had no option but to work with the leftovers since the "better" qualified ones were not available. No, these were the ones He actively sought out; the ones He preferred to work with.

God loves to work with those who have to look to Him for everything. He loves to work with those who come to Him empty. Why? Because their emptiness gives Him the opportunity to fill them with Himself! He loves to work with those who know they are weak because their weakness gives Him the opportunity to become their strength. He loves to work with those who know they are foolish because their foolishness gives Him the opportunity to become their wisdom. He loves to work with those who know they are common because their ordinariness gives Him the opportunity to make them noble.

1 Corinthians 1:30-31, (ESV) reads: *"And because of Him you are in Christ Jesus, who became to us wisdom from God, righteousness, sanctification, and redemption, so that, as it is written, 'Let the one who boasts, boast in the Lord.'"* So contrary to what you may feel, your ordinariness and your inadequacies are the very reason God has chosen you and the very reason He can use you to do some extraordinary things. God will not use any man or woman who is self-dependent. He will only use those who are humble enough to say to Him, "I have no strength, but You; no wisdom, but You; no righteousness, but You. I have nothing to offer You but weakness. But here I am anyway. Use me."

While preaching on this subject recently, I spoke these words under the inspiration of the Holy Spirit:

"Our weaknesses, no matter how great they might be, are but a drop in the ocean of God's strength."

Now, that blesses my heart! God's power will swallow up our weaknesses and make them a non-issue. This means, whatever He has chosen to do through us, He is able to do, in spite of, and sometimes because of, our weaknesses.

God has chosen the weak things of the world. If you think God can't use you, think again!

Affirm Today:

"Lord, I know that I am strong in You. I am ready to be wonderfully used for Your glory. I am confident and excited. My future is great because I trust in You."

Additional Scriptures:

1 Corinthians 1:26-28; 1 Corinthians 1:30; Deuteronomy 7:6; Isaiah 43:4; Zechariah 4:6

Day 18

Spiritual Biology 101

D o you know that you are a three-part being and how each part affects you? Yes, you are an eternal spirit, with a soul, living in a body.

If you have received Jesus as your Lord and Savior, your spirit has been recreated completely. Your inner man, the eternal part of you, is beautiful and perfect, with absolutely no flaw at all. Ephesians 2:10 describes your spirit as God's "workmanship;" literally God's "masterpiece." Your spirit is shielded by God and remains perfect eternally in Christ.

Your recreated spirit is extremely powerful as well. Being joined to Christ and sharing His life, your spirit is equipped with all might and power. In fact, your spirit lives on and functions according to the same power that God manifested when He raised Jesus from the dead. You can do all things through Christ, who shares His strength with you, moment by moment, (Philippians 4:13).

Your body needs to be replaced. Jesus has already paid for your new body, but its delivery is scheduled for some definite date in the future. When Jesus returns, He will deliver our glorified bodies to us. We look with great anticipation to that day when mortality will be swallowed up by immortality. In the meantime, take good care of the one you have and learn how to receive healing through the Word of God, (Proverbs 4:20-22).

The third part of you is your mind, or soul. Your soul consists of your thoughts and imaginations. They in turn produce your emotions and desires. In order to walk in the perfect will of God and experience the blessed life God wants you to have on earth, your soul needs to be renewed, (Romans 12:1-2).

Think of the mind, or soul, as the valve on the faucet that regulates the rate and volume of water that flows from the reservoir through the pipes and into the sink. If the valve is shut, no water enters, even though the reservoir is filled with an abundant supply, far more than is needed. Whether or not the valve is open, and how wide, will determine the results obtained.

This means the soul, or mind, is critical to your earthly experiences. It is the link between all the riches and power of God resident in your recreated spirit and the physical world your body inhabits. Hence, to release the life and power of Christ from your spirit to change your physical world, you must renew your mind.

Your soul has the power to prevent the life-giving power in your spirit from ever reaching your physical body, or it can allow your body to be flooded with the same power that raised Jesus from the dead. If the valve is open and your mind renewed, you'll experience healing, deliverance, anointing, victory, power, joy, prosperity, and more. So, keep it open.

How? Make every effort, depending on the help of the Holy Spirit, to meditate continually on the Word of Grace. Keep beholding Jesus in the Scriptures and keep acknowledging all the good things you already have in Him.

Affirm Today:

"My mind is renewed. I am experiencing healing, deliverance, anointing, victory, power, joy, prosperity, and more."

Additional Scriptures:

Ephesians 2:10; Philippians 4:13; Proverbs 4:20-22; Romans 12:1-2; John 6:63

Day 19

Receive Undeserved Blessings

D o you disqualify yourself from receiving God's blessings because you feel you are not good enough? Do you feel that you have not worked hard enough, been holy enough, prayed long enough, or attended church often enough for God to save your soul and bless your life? If so, then this message is really for you.

> *"God saved you by his grace when you believed. And you can't take credit for this; it is a gift from God. Salvation is not a reward for the good things we have done, so none of us can boast about it. For we are God's masterpiece. He has created us anew in Christ Jesus, so we can do the good things he planned for us long ago."* (Ephesians 2:8-10, NLT)

Please note what those verses say. "Salvation is not a reward for the good things we have done." This means God doesn't forgive our sins, heal our bodies, give us His Spirit, fight our battles and supply our needs because He has seen something good enough in us to deserve His blessings. No matter how hard we try, we can never produce enough holiness on our own to overcome our sinfulness and balance the scales of justice. *"By the deeds of the Law there shall no flesh be justified in His sight"* (Romans 3:20, KJV).

If we can never be good enough to merit even one blessing from God, then are we doomed? Under these circumstances, how can a person ever be saved and blessed? How can God even hear a single prayer?

Here is what the Apostle Paul, by inspiration of the Holy Spirit, has to say to these questions:

> *"You see, at just the right time, when we were still powerless, Christ died for the ungodly. Very rarely will anyone die for a righteous person, though for a good person someone might possibly dare to die. But God demonstrates his own love for us in this: While we were still sinners, Christ died for us."* (Romans 5:6-8, NIV)

Wow! Instead of trying to balance the scales of justice with our good works (which would have been impossible), God balanced it with the sacrificial death of His Son. Jesus' death, not our good works, is what satisfies the righteous requirements of justice and makes it morally possible for a holy God to bless fallen man.

Now, what motivated Jesus to do such an indescribable thing – to take the sinner's place and to sacrifice Himself to save His enemies? What accounts for such "recklessness?" Love, pure love, prodigal love, God's love!

> *"Since we have now been justified by his blood, how much more shall we be saved from God's wrath through him! For if, while we were God's enemies, we were reconciled to him*

through the death of his Son, how much more, having been reconciled, shall we be saved through his life." (Romans 5:9-10, NIV)

What you need to see is that qualifying for God's continual blessings today does not depend on your good works any more than receiving God's initial blessing of salvation did. We are not blessed because we are good. God blesses us because He is good. God is love. All of His blessings are undeserved and unmerited.

Child of God, stop disqualifying yourself from receiving unmerited favor and blessings from God. Instead of thinking God won't bless you because you are not good enough, release God's grace towards you by believing and saying, "If I have been reconciled to God through the death of Jesus, how much more will I be saved (forgiven, healed, prospered) through Jesus' life in me now."

Does this mean you have God's permission to live in sin? *"God forbid! How can we who have died to sin live any longer therein"* (Romans 6:2, KJV)? What it does mean, however, is that your ability to walk in God's blessings and favor is not based on the amount of self-effort you exert, but on the amount of dependence you demonstrate in His love and grace. Never forget, it's not about the strength of your works, not even about the strength of your faith. It's about the strength of God's love and the sufficiency of Jesus' sacrifice. Receive His love and grace freely and then respond to His love by walking in the good works He has ordained for you to walk in.

Affirm Today:

"I have been reconciled to God through the death of Jesus, how much more will I be saved, forgiven, healed, and prospered through Jesus' life in me now."

Additional Scriptures:

Ephesians 2:8-10; Romans 3:20; Romans 5:6-8; Romans 6:2;
Ephesians 1:3

Day 20

Holiness is a Fruit

Are you one of those struggling to live a holy life and experiencing constant condemnation and defeat? Have you been told the problem is that you are not trying hard enough? Or even worse, you are demon possessed? If so, this article will help you.

In Romans 7, the Apostle Paul recounted his miserable failures in his battle with sin. He made up his mind to live a holy life before God, determined to say no to temptation, acknowledged the goodness of the law, and yet found himself time and time again doing the very things he was determined not to do. He wrote:

> *"I find then a law, that evil is present with me, the one who wills to do good. For I delight in the law of God according to the inward man. But I see another law in my members, warring against the law of my mind, and bringing me into captivity to the law of sin which is in my members. O wretched man that I am! Who will deliver me from this body of death?"*
> (Romans 7:21-24)

But that is not the end of the story. Paul discovered the answer to his misery and in the very next verse answered his own question.

> *"I thank God – through Jesus Christ our Lord!*
> *So then, with the mind I myself serve the law*
> *of God; but with the flesh the law of sin."*
> (Romans 7:25)

What had Paul discovered for which he was so thankful? He had discovered that holiness is not a work of the flesh; it is not the product of self-effort and will-power. It is the fruit of union with Jesus Christ. He discovered that while he could not manufacture holiness, he could "bear fruit unto God" through his faith in Christ.

> *"Therefore, my brethren, you also have become*
> *dead to the law through the body of Christ,*
> *that you may be married to another – to Him*
> *who was raised from the dead, that we should*
> *bear fruit to God."* (Romans 7:4)

Child of God, until you make a similar discovery, you will live in constant defeat. You should stop thinking of holiness as something you can accomplish by sheer will-power, much prayer and fasting, and a lot of tears. You can't produce holiness going about it in that manner any more than a woman can produce a baby that way. Children are not manufactured. They are birthed and birthing requires union with a man who carries the seed.

The Scripture declares, you have died to the law and are now "married" to Him who was raised from the dead. Through your spiritual union with Him, He has freely implanted the seed of His life inside of you and the fruit of holiness will spring forth out of the holy seed you have received from Him.

What is your part? As in a marriage, the wife who is intimate with her husband bears his fruit; so your part is to acknowledge His presence in you, enjoy intimacy with Him, and trust Him to cause you to produce His fruit. Holiness is not what you do, but what you allow Jesus to do in you as you fellowship with Him by faith.

Finally, here is my prayer for you.

> *"May the God of peace who brought up our Lord Jesus from the dead, that great Shepherd of the sheep, through the blood of the everlasting covenant, make you complete in every good work to do His will, working in you what is well pleasing in His sight, through Jesus Christ, to whom be glory forever and ever. Amen."* (Hebrews 13:20–21)

Affirm Today:

"I fellowship with Jesus and trust Him by faith to produce His fruit of holiness in me."

Additional Scriptures:

Romans 7:21-25; 1 Corinthians 15:57; Romans 7:4; Hebrews 13:20-21; Philippians 1:6

Day 21

How Grace Empowers You to Overcome

The grace of God is the supernatural tonic you need to live as an overcomer in this world. Grace will abolish the dominion of sin in your life as you surrender to it. It will empower you to say no to all ungodliness and to walk in spiritual authority and power. How?

Here are the three things grace provides that enable you to live victoriously in the Lord;

1. Light

"I have come as a light into the world, that whoever believes in Me should not abide in darkness" (John 12:46).

"But if we walk in the light as He is in the light, we have fellowship with one another, and the blood of Jesus Christ His Son cleanses us from all sin." (1 John 1:7)

"For it is the God who commanded light to shine out of darkness, who has shone in our hearts to give the light of the knowledge of the glory of God in the face of Jesus Christ" (2 Corinthians 4:6).

The message of God's grace will enlighten your heart with the truth concerning how good God is to you and the wonderful things He has prepared for you. It will show you that you are a beloved child of God, "God's workmanship, created in Christ Jesus for good works." It will cause you to see the goodness of God and the goodness of God will lead you to change your mind about Him and about sin. You will begin to see clearly how incredibly wicked and destructive sin is, but how incredibly awesome righteousness is. And the more clearly you see the truth, the more freedom you will enjoy.

2. Love

"And I have declared to them Your name, and will declare it, that the love with which You loved Me may be in them, and I in them" (John 17:26).

"For the love of Christ compels us, because we judge thus: that if One died for all, then all died" (2 Corinthians 5:14).

"That Christ may dwell in your hearts through faith; that you, being rooted and grounded in love, may be able to compre-hend with all the saints what is the width and length and depth and height— to know the love of Christ which passes knowledge; that you may be filled with all the fullness of God" (Ephesians 3:17-19).

The revelation of God's "scandalous" grace floods your heart with love for God and for others. And it will motivate you from within to do the things that please the One who loves you so lavishly. The more grace reveals the love of God to you, the more you will be filled with "the fullness of God." It will produce profound effects on your choices and behavior. Love is far greater than law. Law can only restrain wickedness, but it cannot produce heartfelt obedience. Love, on the other hand, will cause you to be willing to give your life to save the one you love. Law has no power to produce this love, but grace causes this love to be shed abroad in your heart.

3. Life

"Therefore, if anyone is in Christ, he is a new creation; old things have passed away; behold, all things have become new" (2 Corinthians 5:17).

"I have been crucified with Christ; it is no longer I who live, but Christ lives in me; and the life which I now live in the flesh I live by faith in the Son of God, who loved me and gave Himself for me" (Galatians 2:20).

For it is God who works in you both to will and to do for His good pleasure" (Philippians 2:13).

The purpose of God's grace is not to make bad men good, but to make dead men live. Grace imparts life and life overcomes death. The life of Christ within you, not your will-power, is the focus of grace. The grace of God teaches you to rely on this divine life, which you received at salvation, to transform you completely from the inside out. You overcome because you place your faith daily in Christ to live His life for you and through you. You will find yourself hating sin and loving righteousness because "God is working in you both to will and do His good pleasure."

Child of God, the more you immerse yourself in the doctrines of grace, unearned, unmerited undeserved favor; the less you put confidence in the flesh and rest instead in the sufficiency of grace, the more you will experience victory over the world, the flesh and the devil.

Affirm Today:

"I am experiencing the light, love, and life of God's grace. For it is God who is working in me both to will and to do for His good pleasure."

Additional Scriptures:

2 Corinthians 4:6; John 12:46; 1 John 1:7; John 17:26; 2 Corinthians 5:14; 2 Corinthians 5:17; Ephesians 3:17-19; Galatians 2:20; Philippians 2:13

Day 22

You Are God's Gift to the World

D o you need to be needed? I do. I would hate to be unnecessary. Irrelevant. An appendix in the body. Thank God,
this is not the case for me. Nor for you. God would never do
that to us.

> *"But to each one of us grace was given*
> *according to the measure of Christ's gift."*
> (Ephesians 4:7)

To each one, grace was given! He left no one out. He
made sure to include you.

What did He give you? A gift of grace. A gift that makes
you extremely valuable. A gift that empowers you to play a
special role in His body and in this world.

> *"But now God has placed the parts—each one*
> *of them—in the body just as He desired. ...The*
> *eye cannot tell the hand, "I don't need you!"*
> *or in turn the head to the feet, "I don't need*
> *you!"* (1 Corinthians 12:18-21, TLV)

Now, are not the eyes God's gift to the human body? And the hands? And the feet also? Most certainly!

So, what do you become when God graces you with a gift and places you where He wants you to be in the body? You become His gift to the Church. You become His gift to the world!

Child of God, don't listen to the lies the devil places in your mind that make you feel worthless. Don't let anybody convince you that you are unnecessary and insignificant. Remember, you are not only gifted, you are God's gift to the Church. You are His gift to the world.

Now, don't let this make you proud. But do let it make you confident. And grateful.

Affirm Today:

"God has made me a gift, needed and useful. My presence makes a difference and I am grateful."

Additional Scriptures:

1 Corinthians 12:18-21; Ephesians 4:7; Isaiah 6:8; Jeremiah 29:11; Ephesians 2:10

Day 23

Can You Live Holy?

W hen religious minds hear the message of grace preached uncompromisingly, one of the first objections that arises deals with holiness. They wrongly conclude that telling people that Jesus met every requirement of the Law on their behalf and that God has once and for all forgiven them of all their sins, past, present, and future is giving them license to sin. "What about holy living?" they exclaim. "Doesn't the Bible say that without holiness no one will see the Lord?"

Yes, indeed, holiness is an absolute requirement for all saints. Our Father is holy, holy, holy, and He calls us to a life of holiness. And Hebrews 12:14 instructs us to pursue holiness.

But let me pose a question to you. Can you or any human being make anything holy? If according to Jesus, *we are not able to make even one strand of hair on our heads white or black,* (Matthew 5:36) then how much less are we able to produce holiness, no matter how hard we try. Isn't God the only One capable of producing holiness in any shape or form? Now, if this is the case, and indeed it is, then unless God makes us holy, we can never be holy.

If your understanding of Christianity is that God commands us to live a certain way and then expects us to obey, then good luck! Everybody who has tried that approach in their relationship with God has failed miserably. God knows better.

> *"For when we were in the flesh, the sinful desires, aroused by the law, were active in the members of our body to bear fruit for death. But now we have been released from the law, because we have died to what controlled us, so that we may serve in the new life of the Spirit and not under the old written code."*
> (Romans 7:5-6, NET)

Like everything else God desires of us, we get to be holy because He gives it to us in Jesus, and we receive it by faith. **Christianity is Christ in our place**. Christ is our Life. And the good news is God made Him to be our sanctification too! (1 Corinthians 1:30)

Here is a prayer recorded for our benefit in 1 Thessalonians 5:23-24, taken from The Amplified Bible:

> *"And may the God of peace Himself sanctify you through and through [separate you from profane things, make you pure and wholly consecrated to God]; and may your spirit and soul and body be preserved sound and complete [and found] blameless at the coming of our Lord Jesus Christ. Faithful is He Who is calling you [to Himself] and utterly trustworthy, and He will also do it [fulfill His call by hallowing and keeping you]."*

There is *only one way* to live a life that will manifest the fruit of holiness, and that is to trust the faithfulness of the

One who called you to holiness to impart His nature to you and accomplish His will in you.

I love the way Rev. Philip Dunham puts it. "The secret of the Christian life is not "I'll try my best." It is "I'll trust my best."

Child of God, when it comes to holiness, keep in mind that it is *"God who works in you both to will and do His good pleasure"* (Philippians 2:13). **Holiness is not something we offer God; it is something He offers us**. It is not about rules, it is about relationship. And it is not about being in law; it's about being in love!

To live a holy life, place your faith in the only Person who can live this life to do so through you. Don't look to yourself. Look to Christ in you. When we believe, He works.

Affirm Today:

"I affirm 1 Thessalonians 5:23-24 in my life today. Right now, I am sanctified through and through by the God of Peace Himself. I am separated from profane things. I am pure and wholly consecrated to God. My spirit and soul and body are preserved sound and complete. I am blameless. Lord you are faithful and utterly trustworthy. You are doing it and You are keeping me because I am made holy by Your Grace. Amen!"

Additional Scriptures:

Hebrews 12:14; Romans 7:5-6; 1 Corinthians 1:30; 1 Thessalonians 5:23-24; Philippians 2:13

Day 24

The Believers Rest

G od sent Moses to Israel with good news. He was going
to deliver them out of slavery in Egypt and lead them to
a land of rest that flowed with milk and honey. In this land of
rest, He promised His people *"... large and beautiful cities
which you did not build, houses full of all good things, which
you did not fill, hewn-out wells which you did not dig, vine-
yards and olive trees which you did not plant"* (Deuteronomy
6:10–11).

Because of God's grace and favor, they would prosper
effortlessly. They would not have to struggle for blessings.
They could enjoy His rest.

Unfortunately, they failed to enter the rest of God. Instead,
Israel struggled and wandered for forty years in a dry wilderness. Why? They refused to believe! They would not believe
the good news that God had given them a land where everything had been prepared for them in advance, where the work
was finished, a land full of riches to enjoy, a land which just
flowed with His unearned goodness.

Like Israel of old, God has sent us good news. He has sent
Jesus to deliver us from Egypt, the Land of Curses, the place
of bondage and lack; to bring us into the Land of Promises,

where God has already met every need through His Son. He has sent Jesus to bring us into His rest, where we do not have to struggle for blessings, but where we inherit blessings and enjoy favor effortlessly through faith.

Unfortunately, many believers still cannot believe that the work of Jesus on the cross covers every need they have and that it is truly complete and finished. Consequently, you find them struggling hard to produce their healing, prosperity, success and victory. Every day, they are trying to complete a completed work, to finish a finished work and to defeat a defeated devil.

But God wants us to stop struggling to have what He has already provided for us through the finished work of Jesus. He wants us to learn to rest by faith in what He has already done. He wants us to see that in Jesus every need has been met, every promise fulfilled, every battle already won. He wants us to start believing in the sufficiency of His grace toward us and delivered to us on Calvary.

Child of God, the only "work" left for us to do today is to work on our believing. The only "works" necessary now are those that express our gratitude and build our faith in His finished work. Why? Because God has already done all the other work required and has already finished our blessings for us in Jesus!

It was not their shortcomings that kept the children of Israel from entering the Land of Promise. It was their failure to mix God's promises with faith. And today, the only thing that can keep you from enjoying God's best blessings is not believing He has already blessed you with them in Christ.

That is why you must be diligent to let the message of the cross and the grace of God dwell in you richly. Let it fill your heart and renew your mind. By so doing you will enter the believer's rest and start enjoying your own land that flows with milk and honey!

Affirm Today:

"Every need is met in Jesus, every promise fulfilled, every battle already won. I believe and by faith rest."

Additional Scriptures:

Hebrews 4:1-2; Deuteronomy 6:10-11; Mark 9:23; Deuteronomy 28:2; Psalm 119:66

Day 25

Why Jesus Gives Thanks for You

F ive loaves and two fish. Enough to feed a little boy. That was all Jesus had to work with. But that was all He needed. All He needed to feed more than five thousand men. Amazing!

> *"Then Jesus lifted up His eyes, and seeing a great multitude coming toward Him, He said to Philip, "Where shall we buy bread, that these may eat?" But this He said to test him, for He Himself knew what He would do. Philip answered Him, "Two hundred denarii worth of bread is not sufficient for them, that every one of them may have a little." One of His disciples, Andrew, Simon Peter's brother, said to Him, "There is a lad here who has five barley loaves and two small fish, but what are they among so many?" Then Jesus said, 'Make the people sit down.' Now there was much grass in the place. So the men sat down, in number about five thousand."* (John 6:5-10)

You can sense frustration in both Philip and Andrew. Philip says, "The need is too great; don't even try!" Andrew says, "The supply is too small; why even bother?" Jesus says, "It is enough. Get ready for a miracle."

> *"And Jesus took the loaves, and when He had given thanks He distributed them to the disciples, and the disciples to those sitting down; and likewise of the fish, as much as they wanted."* (John 6:11)

Jesus gave thanks. I love this. They were few, they were small, and they were weak, yet He accepted them! And then, He gave thanks for them! Why? He knew what they would become in His hands, what He would make of them.

Child of God, do you realize what this means? If He gave thanks for five loaves and two fish, just imagine how much He gives thanks for you! If He could feed more than five thousand men with just five loaves and two fish, just imagine what He knows He can do with your life!

Others may look at you and think you are no better than a little boy's lunch. Nothing good or great will come out of you. Too small, too weak, too little. Nothing to get excited about, to give thanks for.

But Jesus thinks differently. He gives thanks for you. Why? You are in His hands. And He knows what He is making of you. He knows what you are becoming. He knows the blessing you are destined to be to many.

Now, if Jesus is thankful for you, child of God, it's time for you to be thankful yourself – for Him, for you, for the destiny He has planned for you. Stop saying, "I'm too small, I'm too weak," and start boldly declaring, "I'm in Jesus' hands and He is rejoicing over me. I have everything I need. I am more than enough in Him. My destiny is great. Thank You, Father."

Truly, this is the day the Lord has made. Let's rejoice and be glad in it!

Affirm Today:

"Jesus, I am happy in Your hands. I am delighted that You rejoice over me. I now possess more than enough for my life, my family and every good work ahead. My destiny is planned and it is great! Thank You, Jesus!"

Additional Scriptures:

John 6:5-11; 1 Peter 2:9; Philippians 4:13; 2 Peter 1:3; 2 Timothy 1:9

Day 26

God Freely Gives to You All Things

It's unfortunate that so many Christians have not grasped the extent of the Father's love and how eager He is to meet their needs. They beg, they cry, they sacrifice, all in an effort to "get" God to hear their prayers. To persuade Him to meet their needs. But is any of this necessary?

Consider the following verses:

> *"Do not fear, little flock, for it is your Father's good pleasure to give you the kingdom."* (Luke 12:32)

> *"Look at the birds of the air, for they neither sow nor reap nor gather into barns; yet your heavenly Father feeds them. Are you not of more value than they?"* (Matthew 6:26)

> *"What then shall we say to these things? If God is for us, who can be against us? He who did not spare His own Son, but delivered Him up for us all, how shall He not with Him also freely give us all things?"* (Romans 8:31-32)

God's love for you is astonishing. And because of His great love for you, He will withhold no good thing from you. Neither do you need to persuade Him with your tears and good works to convince Him to meet your needs.

In fact, if you look closely at Romans 8:31-32, you will discover an amazing truth. God did not spare His own Son, but delivered Him up for you. And when did He do this? When you were an unholy, rebellious sinner!

But look again. What else does it say? God freely gives you all things. All things you need for life and godliness, God freely – with absolutely no cost to you, gives to you! And when did He do so? "With Jesus," two-thousand years ago! God took care of all your needs when He delivered up Jesus for you two-thousand years ago.

Child of God, never doubt your Heavenly Father's love for you, how eager He is to help you, and His commitment to seeing to it that your needs are met. There is no need to beg for what He already has given you. Instead of worrying, meditate on His Word, believe His promises, give thanks, and rest in His love.

Affirm Today:

"It is my Father's good pleasure to give me the kingdom. I have everything I need for life and godliness because of His amazing love."

Additional Scriptures:

Romans 8:31-32;,Luke 12:32; Matthew 6:26; Luke 12:28; Philippians 4:19

Day 27

An Amazing Truth

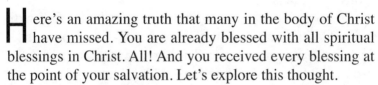

H ere's an amazing truth that many in the body of Christ have missed. You are already blessed with all spiritual blessings in Christ. All! And you received every blessing at the point of your salvation. Let's explore this thought.

A few years ago, I purchased a car for my wife. Even though you may have never seen that car, would you ask me whether the car has four tires on it? Of course not! People do not purchase new cars and then return to purchase the tires for the car separately. New cars come with the four tires already attached! Similarly, if I told you I owned a German Shepherd, would you ask me if it had a tail? No, because you would know that German Shepherds are dogs born with tails.

Likewise, when we received Jesus as Savior we received everything we would ever need for life and godliness, simultaneously. Salvation came to us with every spiritual blessing attached. It came with forgiveness of sins, healing of diseases, and peace of mind, wisdom, protection, fruitfulness and good success. To have Jesus in your life and still think that you lack any blessing is as silly as buying a new car and wondering whether it comes with four tires attached. Of course it does! And of course you have all things in Christ!

> *"For in Him dwells all the fullness of the Godhead bodily; and you are complete in Him, who is the head of all principality and power."* (Colossians 2:9-10)

In Him you are complete! Lack nothing. Full. Whole. Having all necessary or appropriate parts. Wow!

The Scriptures teach that Jesus redeemed us from every curse when He Himself became a curse for us on the cross. When did Jesus receive these curses? The minute He accepted our sins. The curses that came upon Him were attached to the sins He took upon Himself. In order to be cursed with every curse, all that was necessary was for Him to take upon Himself our sins.

But the Good News is that in order to be blessed with every blessing, all that was necessary was for you to take upon you His righteousness. The blessings are attached to the gift of righteousness. They came with salvation.

> *"For if by the one man's offense death reigned through the one, much more those who receive abundance of grace and of the gift of righteousness will reign in life through the One, Jesus Christ."* (Romans 5:17)

Child of God, you do not need to wonder whether God will forgive you, heal you, or provide all of your needs. He already has. And you do not need to wonder whether you have enough faith to obtain your blessings. Jesus already obtained them for you and God has already given them to you.

Are you wondering what your part is? It's simple. Stop trying to get through self-effort what God has already given you freely by grace. And start thanking Him for and confessing aloud that you are righteous and blessed with every spiritual blessing in Christ Jesus. Only believe and you will see the glory of God.

Affirm Today:

"I am blessed and I am highly favored by God. Everything I will ever need has been given to me. I celebrate what is happening in my life. Overflowing joy is mine and I am complete."

Additional Scriptures:

Colossians 2:9-10; Romans 5:17; Deuteronomy 28:8; Psalm 84:11; 2 Samuel 22:33

Day 28

Who Has Bewitched You?

When Apostle Paul asked Christians the question in Galatians 3:1, "Who has bewitched you?", he did not have in mind African witch doctors, Haitian voodoo men, or American witches flying around on broomsticks. He was referring to religionists, the Judaizers, who shortly after Paul led the Galatians to Christ, began to oppose Paul's preaching of salvation by grace through faith, apart from works. And the Galatian Christians were being persuaded to believe their message.

Paul was shocked that the Galatians were so *"...quickly deserting him who called you in the grace of Christ and are turning to a different gospel, not that there is another one... but even if we or an angel from heaven should preach to you a gospel contrary to the one we preached to you, let him be accursed"* (Galatians 1:6-8, ESV). Those are strong words – "let him be accursed!"

What was this "different gospel" being preached that elicited such outrage from the Apostle? The religionists were preaching that faith in Christ alone, apart from the law, was not enough to make a person righteous in God's sight. They preached that while believing in Christ was essential to salvation, a person still had to contribute his own works to what

Christ had done in order to be righteous in God's sight. That is, salvation was a combination of Jesus' work for us and our work for Him – a mixture of grace and law.

That sounds good, but this was what Paul rejected so vehemently. You see, this mixture of grace and law is deadly. It neutralizes both grace and law, and makes the cure for sin ineffective. It's similar to taking two different medicines, one for high blood pressure and the other for low blood pressure, at the same time. The two will counteract each other and the patient will not receive the benefit of either. He could die as a result of trying to cure himself by taking both medicines simultaneously.

Unfortunately, this is what too many well-meaning Christians are trying to do. Not knowing the purpose of the law, they are trying to mix law and grace to solve the sin problem. In the process, neither law nor grace is effective in them, and they end up living defeated lives. Many die never experiencing the victorious life Christ makes available to all who believe in Him, still suffering continuously under the condemnation of the law.

The law is good when it is used for its intended purpose. But its purpose is not to justify us before God, to bless us, or give life to us, and trying to use it for any of those reasons will prevent grace from taking effect in us fully. Listen to Apostle Paul as he talks about the law.

> *"By works of the law no one will be justified...*
> *For all who rely on the works of the law are*
> *under a curse...For if a law had been given*
> *that could give life, then righteousness would*
> *indeed be by the law."* (Galatians 2:16; 3:10;
> 3:21, ESV)

Did you hear this – all who are trying to be righteous or blessed through keeping the law are under a curse! No law can give life! The reason all who rely on the law are under a curse is because the law sets such a high standard that to be blessed under it, you have to obey it perfectly. Break just one and it curses you! Just one and you die! Ask Adam and Eve. So anyone who is depending on their law-keeping to recommend him or her to God for blessing is in big trouble. The law will condemn us every time!

Why then was the law given? Not to save us, not to justify us, but to reveal our need for faith in the *grace of God!*

> *"Now we know that whatever the law says it speaks to those who are under the law, so that every mouth may be stopped, and the whole world may be held accountable to God. For by works of the law no human being will be justified in his sight, since through the law comes knowledge of sin."* (Romans 3:19-20, ESV)

> *"Now before faith came, we were held captive under the law…So then the law was our guardian until Christ came, in order that we might be justified by faith. But now that faith has come, we are no longer under a guardian, for in Christ Jesus you are all sons of God, through faith."* (Galatians 3:23-26, ESV)

You see, the law is a guardian. It has a role to play until we come to Christ. But once we come to Christ, we no longer need to be under a guardian – the law. If through the law, we have seen how exceedingly sinful we are, how our own righteousness is as filthy rags next to God's, and therefore have become totally dependent upon Christ for our righteousness, then the law has accomplished its purpose in our lives. Henceforth, like Paul, we must consider our own attempts at being righteous by keeping the law as rubbish that we may *"be found in Him, not having a righteousness of my own that comes from the law, but that which comes through faith in Christ"* (Philippians 3:9, ESV).

Do not dilute the power of grace in your life by trying to earn righteousness from God by keeping commandments. Believe that God has made Him *"who knew no sin to be sin for you that you might be made the righteousness of God in Him"* (2 Corinthians 5:21). Believe you are *"saved by grace through faith, apart from works; it is a gift from God"* (Ephesians 2:8-9).

Isn't this a license to sin? No! Does this mean you can now live as you please? Yes! But there is a catch! The grace of God will teach you to say no to ungodliness (Titus 2:11-12).

You see, when a person receives salvation by faith in God's grace, God doesn't just forgive him, He changes him. He puts His Holy Spirit inside of that person. He regenerates him and makes him a new creature in Christ. He gives him new desires.

And so he can now live as he pleases. But the person saved by grace will find that a life of sin and disobedience no longer pleases him! What pleases him now will be to please the One who saved him by His grace. He will hate sin more under grace than He ever did under law. And the more he relies on the grace of God for righteousness, the more he will hate sin. Holiness will become a way of life, not in order to establish his own righteousness, but as the fruit of the righteousness God has given him by grace through faith.

Do not allow yourself to be bewitched by bringing yourself back under the condemnation of the law and trying to add to the righteousness God has given you in Christ. You are saved by grace through faith, apart from your works. Believe this, and then let the grace of God change you from the inside out.

Affirm Today:

"I am saved by grace through faith, apart from my works. The grace of God is changing me from the inside out."

Additional Scriptures:

Galatians 3:1; Titus 2:11-12; Ephesians 2:8-9; Philippians 3:9; Galatians 1:6; Galatians 2:16; Galatians 3:10; Galatians 3:21; Romans 3:19-20; Galatians 3:23-26

Day 29

Where Are Your Blessings?

Let me tell you where your blessings are.

D o you remember your junior high Science class? Then you know, for thousands of years, water has been moving in a cycle, from earth to the air and back to the earth again. During this water cycle, its chemical composition, H_2O, does not change, but the form it exists in does. It can go from being a gas, to a liquid, to a solid. That's right – water can exist as a gas, but under the right conditions can become as solid as ice. What does this have to do with your blessings? A lot! Read on.

Ephesians 1:3 tells us that God has blessed us with all spiritual blessings in the heavenly places in Christ Jesus. Notice, He has already blessed us with every blessing we will ever need. God has fulfilled every promise, having provided righteousness, health, peace and godly prosperity for us already. You already have what you think you lack.

"But if so, why don't I see them? Where are these blessings you are talking about?"

Remember the water cycle? Water can exist as an invisible gas, but under the right conditions change into solid ice. While in its gaseous state, it exists, but is unobservable to the senses. But it's there, as much water as it will ever be!

You would be wrong to conclude no water is in the air just because it is invisible. Create the right set of conditions and it will manifest itself to you.

Your blessings are right there, in Christ, in you. They exist in their spirit form, but they are as real as water in its gaseous state. Don't be fooled into thinking that just because they are unobservable they are not already present with you. They are there because God declared it so. Create the right set of conditions in your heart and they will manifest themselves to you. Like water, God gives those blessings the power to change their form, to go from being just spiritual to being emotional and physical. To becoming the type of blessing you can feel and touch!

Water needs cold or heat to change form. And spiritual blessings need faith in God's Word and patience to materialize.

> *"Therefore I say to you, whatever things you ask when you pray, believe that you receive them, and you will have them."* (Mark 11:24)

The woman with the issue of blood said, *"If I but touch the hem of his garments, I will be healed"* (Matthew 9:21). She believed her healing, though invisible, was already present in Him. She released her faith with her words and her health materialized; instantly, in her case.

Are you asking God to bless you? You are too late. He already has! Therefore, when you pray, do not beg God to bless you. Instead, believe He has already blessed you and release faith out of your mouth with your words. Then continue to confess God's Word, to give thanks, to believe knowing that the blessing which today exists in spirit form will surely manifest "tomorrow," in the form of a blessing that is as solid as ice! It may not happen instantly, but it will, if you faint not.

Now that you know where your blessings are, enjoy!

Affirm Today:

"I expect miracles in my life. Your wondrous love and grace manifests in my life in wonderful unexpected ways."

Additional Scriptures:

Ephesians 1:3; Mark 11:24; Matthew 9:20-22; John 1:16; Acts 20:32

Day 30

All Your Needs

John Calvin was one of the greatest theologians who ever lived. He said, "I gave up all for Christ and what have I found? I have found everything in Christ."

Many years earlier the Apostle Paul wrote, *"My God shall supply all your needs according to his riches in glory by Christ Jesus"* (Philippians 4:19). That is a promise you can go to the bank on!

Now, our needs and our wants do not always match. I may want to play outdoors when what I need to do is to work indoors. I may want ice cream when what I need are some steamed vegetables and brown rice. I may want to get married to a particular person because I think that will fulfill me when what I need is to learn how to be fulfilled through my relationship with Christ. I may want people to serve me when what I need is to serve others.

Satan has managed to confuse many of us into not knowing the difference. So we buy things we don't need, with money we don't have, to impress people we don't even like. We try to keep up with the Jones family, but when we finally catch up with them, they refinance."

Beloved, God loves us too much to give us everything we want, but He loves us too much not to provide everything we need.

Bartimaeus, the blind beggar, sitting by the roadside as Jesus was leaving Jericho found this to be true. *"Jesus, Son of David, have mercy on me,"* he cried. Such a simple prayer. Just a few words. But all that was required to get his need met! *"What would you have me to do for you?"* Jesus asked. *"Lord,"* he replied, *"that I might receive my sight"* (Mark 10:47-51). *"Go your way,"* said Jesus, *"Your faith has made you well."* And immediately he received his sight!"

Beloved, what is it that you really need? What would you have Jesus do for you? God has promised to supply all your needs through Him, so just like Bartimaeus did, tell Jesus your need. Believe. Then, with childlike faith, begin to declare with confidence; my God is supplying all my needs according to His riches in glory. And He will!

Affirm Today:

"I am learning to trust You Lord. My eyes are on You for You are my supply. I have every resource for health, wealth and happiness. I am walking in faith trusting You every step of the way."

Additional Scriptures:

Mark 10:46-52; Philippians 4:19; Colossians 1:27; Ephesians 1:18-19; Matthew 6:33

Day 31

Motivated by Love

The greatest commandment is that you should love the Lord with all your heart. It is clear that God wants our hearts. He wants our relationship with Him and our service to Him to be from the heart and motivated by love. One of God's major complaints against Israel was they served him with their mouths, but their hearts were far from him. God wanted their hearts. And this is one of the problems with the law – it can produce fear of God, but it cannot produce love for God.

Now there are those who feel that the reason there is so much sinning going on in the body of Christ is because there is not enough preaching about hell and damnation. They feel that believers need to hear more about curses and judgment in order to obey God. That if people are not made to be afraid of what God will do to them if they do not obey him, they will not serve him. I do not believe this for one moment.

And this is why:

Firstly, what does this say about God? It suggests that the only reason people serve God is because they are forced to, not because God is good; not because He is worthy. If this is so, what kind of God is He? Do you mean God is so undesirable that given a choice, men will always choose to serve the devil? I cannot believe this. I am convinced that God is so good and so wise and powerful that anybody who gets to know Him for whom He really is will fall in love with Him and gladly serve Him.

Secondly, I do not believe God wants anybody serving Him because of the fear of what will happen if they do not. God gets absolutely no glory out of such service because it is not free and from the heart; it is forced and is merely external. Perhaps, I believe this about God because that's how I would feel about anybody serving me out of fear. I would rather a person not serve me at all than for him or her to serve me only because they are afraid of what I will do to him or her if they do not. So, if the only reason a person serves God is because he or she is afraid of going to hell, I believe that that person's service grieves God and brings Him no joy.

Thirdly, love is a far more powerful and noble motivation than fear and people will do far more because of love than they will ever do because of law. If you serve only because it's the law, then you still are thinking only of yourself and will try to get away with whatever you can, if you can do so, without being caught or punished. The person, however, who serves because of love is deeply motivated to do good for the sake of the other, and therefore needs no law to do what is good and right.

Now, that's the type of service God delights in and that is the type of relationship He desires to have with us. And this can never be produced in a heart motivated by fear of judgment. It is only possible in a heart full of faith and love.

That's why God wants you to know the height, breadth, length, and depth of His love for you; that's why He wants you to know His love that passes understanding!

Child of God, here is a prayer from the Spirit for you. Pray this for yourself. Pray this for the saints. It holds the key to experiencing the fullness of God for your life today.

Affirm Today:

> *"For this reason I bow my knees to the Father of our Lord Jesus Christ, from whom the whole family in heaven and earth is named, that He would grant me, according to the riches of His glory, to be strengthened with might through His Spirit in the inner man, that Christ may dwell in my heart through faith; that I, being rooted and grounded in love, may be able to comprehend with all the saints what is the width and length and depth and height—to know the love of Christ which passes knowledge; that I may be filled with all the fullness of God. Now to Him who is able to do exceedingly abundantly above all that we ask or think, according to the power that works in us, to Him be glory in the church by Christ Jesus to all generations, forever and ever. Amen."* (Ephesians 3:14-21)

Additional Scriptures:

Ephesians 3:14-21; Romans 8:35-39; Deuteronomy 7:9; John 14:23; Romans 5:8

Day 32

Blessed Assurance

"*If you love me, you will keep my commandments*" (John 14:15). Does this sound like a warning to you? Does it cause you to question your relationship with God and how He feels about you? Does it feel like you are still under the Law? I used to feel this way, but I don't any longer. Why?

Read the entire chapter of John 14, and you will see that it is all about comfort and assurance. Jesus is getting His disciples ready for His departure and He is assuring them that all will be well. He is not going to let them live like orphans. He assures them that they will never be alone and He will supply all of their needs. His intent is to comfort them, not scare them!

This is the context in which He is speaking when He brings up the subject of obedience. He does not want them to be worried about keeping His commandments either. He wants to encourage them, not frighten them.

So He assures them if they love Him, they will obey Him. If love is the root, obedience will be the inevitable fruit. And, here is the good news, He had a plan for rooting them in His love!

He promised to send them a personal Helper, the Holy Spirit, who would live inside of them continually. His job would be to guide them into all truth and show them what Jesus wants them to do in every situation. And through His ministry of revelation, the Holy Spirit will fill their hearts with love for Him. And since obedience flows out from love, this divinely produced love will cause them to keep His Word, effortlessly.

> *"And hope does not disappoint, because the love of God has been poured out within our hearts through the Holy Spirit who was given to us."* (Romans 5:5, NASB)

Here is the bottom line. Instead of being frightened that you will not be able to keep the commandments, be assured that the love of God has been shed abroad in your heart by the Holy Spirit. And that the love He wants from you is the love He supplies to you. And the love He supplies to you will cause you to produce the fruit of obedience that He wants from you.

"If ye love me, you will keep my commandments." Not a warning; a promise!

Affirm Today:

"I love You Jesus and will keep Your commandments. This is Your promise to me and my blessed assurance."

Additional Scriptures:

John 14:15; Romans 5:5; John 14:18; John 14:27; Romans 8:28

Day 33

How to Love

Just a few hours before His death, Jesus called His team together and said, "A new commandment I give you." What was it? Not be more committed, be more zealous, or be more dedicated. But "Love one another as I have loved you." He did not give them Ten Commandments, or five, just one.

Love was to be the distinguishing mark of His disciples – their logo. *"By this all will know that you are my disciples."* By this kind of love – "as I have loved you."

People use the word "love" for so many things today, it can be confusing. But Jesus took the time to make sure His disciples understood exactly what He was talking about. Before telling them what He wanted them to do, He exemplified it. He showed them by His actions how they were to live and love.

> *"Now before the Feast of the Passover…Jesus, knowing that the Father had given all things into His hands, and that He had come from God and was going to God, rose from supper and laid aside His garments, took a towel and girded Himself. After that, He poured water*

> *into a basin and began to wash the disciples'*
> *feet, and to wipe them with the towel with*
> *which He was girded."* (John 13:1-5)

He was showing them what it means to "love...as I have loved you." He was demonstrating it for all to see.

> *"So when He had washed their feet, taken His*
> *garments, and sat down again, He said to them,*
> *"Do you know what I have done to you? You*
> *call Me Teacher and Lord, and you say well,*
> *for so I am. If I then, your Lord and Teacher,*
> *have washed your feet, you also ought to wash*
> *one another's feet."* (John 13:12-14)

Loving as Jesus loves can be dirty work. And smelly at times, but it is spiritually very rewarding!

> *"For I have given you an example, that you*
> *should do as I have done to you. Most assur-*
> *edly, I say to you, a servant is not greater*
> *than his master; nor is he who is sent*
> *greater than he who sent him. If you know*
> *these things, blessed are you if you do them."*
> (John 13:15-17)

Without words, but by His works, He preached to them one of His most important sermons. And He did so while going through the most difficult period of His life, using only a basin and a towel. He showed them love. And then assured them that if they choose to live and love like this, they will be richly blessed.

Now, here is an important point to note. How can you love as He loves you unless you first know His love for you personally? So the place to begin is with knowing how totally in love Jesus is with you and how He Himself "washes your feet" daily. The more clearly you can see Him "washing your feet" today, the more effortlessly you will wash the feet of others.

Child of God, you can live and love as He. All you need is a basin and a towel and some hands that are willing to wash dirty feet. And of course, a daily revelation of how much Jesus loves you!

Now, go wash some "dirty feet" today, just for the fun of it, and watch God change lives through you!

Affirm Today:

"Jesus, all will know that I am Your disciple because I will love others as You have loved me."

Additional Scriptures:

John 13:34-35; John 13:1-5; John 13:14; Titus 3:3-5; Deuteronomy 7:9

Day 34

How Can Jesus Be God?

S ome say He's a good man, a prophet, perhaps the greatest and most holy man to ever live. But they say, He's not God. Are they right? Can He be good, holy and great, and yet not be who He claimed to be?

Consider this rational exercise, the trilemma argument, popularized by C. S. Lewis, to determine the deity of Jesus:

Jesus claimed to be God. He permitted His disciples to call Him their Lord and God. He even allowed them to worship Him.

Since Jesus claimed to be God and accepted worship, He has left us with only three rational options concerning His person:

1. Jesus knew He was not God, but claimed to be anyway. That would make Him a deceiver. He's a liar.

2. Jesus thought He was God, but He was wrong. That would mean He was deceived. He's a lunatic.

3. Jesus was God. That would mean He was neither deceived, or a deceiver. He's the Lord.

These are the only three options He gives us. We cannot call Him a good man if He is a liar, and we cannot call Him a wise man if He is a lunatic. Either we reject Him as a fool or renounce Him as a devil, or we must accept His claim and revere Him as God. What we cannot do with any integrity is to say He deceived multitudes by claiming to be God and yet call Him a holy and good man. What we cannot do is say He was deluded and yet call Him a wise and great prophet. If He lied about being God, then He's not holy and good. If He was deluded, then He's not wise and great.

But we are left with one other option. If He was too good to be a liar, and too wise to be a lunatic, then He must have told the truth to His disciples. He is more than a great moral teacher and more than a major prophet. He is the divine Son of God!

Now, He did not only claim to be divine, He arose from the dead to prove it! If you say He did not rise from the dead, then tell me what happened to His body? If you say His disciples moved it, please tell me why these very ordinary men would do such a foolish thing. Why would eleven men invent a lie to be beaten and imprisoned for, to be stoned to death for, and to be sawed in half for, to be crucified upside-down for? That would make no sense. When men lie, it is to avoid suffering, not ensure it!

The grave is empty, not because the disciples hid His body, and certainly not because the Roman soldiers or Jewish religious leaders moved it. That would have been the last thing they would ever do. The grave is empty because Jesus told the truth: He is God.

If Jesus is who He claimed to be, and He is, then the most important relationship anyone can have is with Him. Then paying attention to everything else He said is the wisest thing anyone can do. Then refusing to accept Him as one's personal Lord and Savior is the greatest mistake one could ever make!

Jesus is God. What will you do with Him? What will you let Him do with you?

Here is the Good News. "For God so loved the world that He gave His only begotten Son that whosoever believes in Him should not perish, but have everlasting life." You may believe on Him now, receive Him as your Lord and God today, and be saved forever. Wow!

I pray you do.

Affirm Today:

"Jesus, I know You are Lord and You are God. I believe that You died on the cross for my sins. I accept You into my life right now as my personal Savior. I surrender all I am to You. I release the past and I welcome living my new life in You."

Additional Scriptures:

John 3:16; John 1:1-3; John 1:12; Matthew 1:21; 1 John 3:23; John 1:17

Day 35

Is Christianity the Only True Religion?

R eligions abound, all types, each claiming to be true. With so many religions in the world, how can one be sure which one, if any, is true? One thing is certain, they cannot be all equally valid and they cannot all be from God. Why? They contradict each other. If God authored more than one of them, He would have to be schizophrenic.

Either they are all false, or only one, at the most, is true. So which one, if any, is right? My answer is unequivocally Christianity. I respect all people and all faiths, but I believe in only one divinely inspired message and that is the Gospel of Jesus Christ.

Briefly, this is why I find Christianity to be true:

1. The uniqueness of its Source: Jesus. No other founder of any of the world's great religions made the types of claims Jesus made. He claimed to be the Son of God, to have the power to forgive sins, and to be both the Savior and Judge of the world. And He's the only One who died and rose again and presented Himself alive to more than five-hundred eyewitnesses afterwards! Jesus stands alone, in a class by Himself.

2. The uniqueness of its Scriptures: The Bible. Like no other holy book ever written, the Bible is filled with detailed prophecies of future events, places and people predicted hundreds of years in advance. It even predicts long before Christ, the name of the little town He would be born in, His flight to Egypt, the exact manner of His death, and His resurrection. No other book ever written contains so many fulfilled prophecies. The accuracy of hundreds of prophecies points to a divine source and proves divine authorship. The Bible stands alone, in a class by itself.

3. The uniqueness of its Solution: The Cross. All of the great religions have one thing in common – they recognize an internal problem in human beings that have resulted in a break down in their relationship with the Divine. To fix the problem, except for Christianity, all of them offer a system of laws to follow and rituals to perform. Within their systems, the onus is on man to do his best to make up for his deficiency and hope it suffices. Christianity differs. Instead of placing the onus on man, it looks to God for the solution. Instead of asking for a sacrifice, it provides the sacrifice. Instead of providing a system, it provides a Savior. The Cross stands alone, in a class by itself.

Is Christianity the only true religion? I am convinced it is. I am not being intolerant; I am just being honest. And here are Jesus' own words to that effect:

Jesus said to him, *"I am the way, and the truth, and the life; no one comes to the Father but through Me"* (John 14:6, NASB).

Either He's a liar, a lunatic, or The Lord!

I invite you to consider Christianity's claims and accept its Savior. Why not invite Him into your life today?

Affirm Today:

"Jesus is the way, and the truth, and the life; I come to God through Him. And I am grateful."

Additional Scriptures:

John 4:16; Mark 1:14-15; Romans 3:3-4; Psalm 119:66; Isaiah 43:10

Day 36

Did Jesus Come to Make Bad Men Good?

C ontrary to what many religious people believe, Jesus did not come to make bad men good. He came to make dead men live. That is why Christianity is not religion. It is not self-improvement. It is not about you doing your best to be holy. Christianity is Life. It is God's Life, imparted to you, working powerfully in you, flowing miraculously through you.

God said to Adam, the day you sin you will die. Adam sinned and death entered. And death spread to all men. So you see, the problem is not merely that men are bad. It is far worse than that! Sinners are dead.

> *"Therefore, just as through one man sin entered the world, and death through sin, and thus death spread to all men, because all sinned ... Nevertheless death reigned from Adam to Moses, even over those who had not sinned according to the likeness of the transgression of Adam, who is a type of Him who was to come."* (Romans 5:12, 14)

It should be obvious. Dead men cannot do good. Dead men cannot obey. Dead men cannot be holy. Dead men cannot contribute to their salvation. Think about it, you who make salvation a matter of man's works. What good work could dead Lazarus have done to help himself stop the process of decay that was at work in his lifeless body? How could the Ten Commandments have helped him?

There is only one way for dead men to come alive; only one way to get movement and growth again. That is for life to enter them. There is only one way for sinners who are already dead in trespasses and sins to be holy. It is for the life of Jesus, eternal life, to enter them.

And this is what salvation is all about. It is receiving His Life – in us, from the Father, through the Son, by the Spirit, through faith. We live because He is alive in us.

> *"But God, who is rich in mercy, because of His great love with which He loved us, even when we were dead in trespasses, made us alive together with Christ (by grace you have been saved), and raised us up together, and made us sit together in the heavenly places in Christ Jesus."* (Ephesians 2:4-6)

Christians are not people trying to live for God, trying to do good. Christians are already alive in the Spirit. They are holy vessels containing the Life of God and spiritual branches manifesting the Life of God. We are fruit-bearers, not religious "do-gooders." We simply experience and effortlessly manifest the good fruit of His Life more and more as we learn to rest in His finished work and behold His glory.

Child of God, our salvation is truly the work of God. We are saved not by our love for God, but by His love for us. The Father conceived it, the Son achieved it, the Spirit revealed it; we received it. Let's celebrate it!

Affirm Today:

"I am alive with Christ, raised up and seated with Him in heavenly places. My salvation is the work of God. I am saved by His love for me and I celebrate it."

Additional Scriptures:

Romans 5:12,14; Romans 3:23; Ephesians 2:4-6; John 1:16-17; Matthew 7:13-14

Day 37

Got Trouble?

Here is one thing I can tell you without ever having met you. No matter who you are, or where you live, at this point in your life, you are either in trouble, just coming out of trouble, or on your way into trouble. I'm sure I am right. And I am not even a prophet! I know so because earth is fallen and the devil is real.

But do not despair. Do not be afraid either. Divine help is available. Listen to these encouraging words from 1 Peter 5:6-7:

> *"Therefore humble yourselves under the*
> *mighty hand of God, that He may exalt you*
> *in due time, casting all your care upon Him,*
> *for He cares for you."*

You will have trouble in this world, but God does not want trouble to have you. He does not want you to be overcome by worries and anxieties. He doesn't want you depressed, or defeated. And that's why He invites you to "cast" your troubles upon Him.

The word translated "casting" in this verse means "to throw upon; to unload." So, instead of you dealing with your troubles yourself, in your strength, God asks that you throw all your care [the whole of your care, all your anxieties, all your concerns, once and for all] on Him! He invites you to say to Him, "Here, God, You handle this, all of this, because I can't."

Now, why does God want you to cast all of your cares upon Him and let Him deal with them for you? Peter gives us two reasons. Firstly, because, "He cares for you." In this verse, the word translated "care" is *mérimna*, and it means "to be anxious about" or "to be concerned." God does not worry, and He is never anxious, but if He could be, it would be right to say that He is worried about you and extremely concerned about your welfare.

The second reason God wants you to give Him your troubles is because He knows He is more than able to handle any problem you put in His hands. His hands, the verse says, are "mighty." This speaks of His "great and impressive strength and power." With so much strength and power at His disposal, God has far more than He needs to carry your load.

Child of God, in this world you will have trouble, but do not let trouble have you. When trouble comes, learn to hear the voice of your Heavenly Father beckoning you to cast all of your cares upon Him. Then, humble yourself by giving Him your troubles. Drop them off at His doorsteps. Place them firmly in His hands. Let Him have them, every last one of them, knowing He loves you infinitely.

And since you also know His hands are mighty, you can be confident He is more than able to take care of you. At the right time, just like the verse says, God will exalt you. Just like He promised.

Affirm Today:

"God is more than able to handle the problems in my life. I confidently place them all in His mighty hands."

Additional Scriptures:

1 Peter 5:6-7; John 16:33; Psalm 31:15; Psalm 37:40; Psalm 9:9

Day 38

When Trouble Comes

N one of us would deny that we are living under incredible pressure. Sometimes life seems like one continuous migraine headache. So, how do you deal with troubling, stressful situations? Do you lose your ability to sleep, turn to food, become discouraged, or get angry? If your response to stressors is inadequate, physical, emotional, or spiritual illness results. You may experience burn-out, loss of motivation, depression, and even feel suicidal. Every hour, every day, on average, three persons commit suicide in the United States because they cannot cope with stress.

Instead of allowing trouble and stress to destroy us, we can turn to God and enlist His help. How? 1 Peter 5:6-11 provides the answer:

> *"Therefore humble yourselves under the mighty hand of God, that He may exalt you in due time, casting all your care upon Him, for He cares for you. Be sober, be vigilant; because your adversary the devil walks about like a roaring lion, seeking whom he may devour. Resist him, steadfast in the faith,*

knowing that the same sufferings are experi-
enced by your brotherhood in the world. But
may the God of all grace, who called us to His
eternal glory by Christ Jesus, after you have
suffered a while, perfect, establish, strengthen,
and settle you. To Him be the glory and the
dominion forever and ever. Amen."

These verses were addressed to Christians living during a period of great persecution. You can imagine the kind of stress they were under each day as they were being arrested, beaten, imprisoned and killed. But they coped successfully with stress, and you can too, by following God's instructions for dealing with trouble:

1. Submit to God. (vs. 6) The first thing you should do when under pressure is to submit yourself and the situation to God totally. Why? Because God gives grace (power) to the humble. To submit is to place yourself completely under His authority and protection and to say to Him, "I accept whatever You want to teach me in this situation and whatever You want to do for me and through me." God is good and has promised to make all things work out for our good, if we place them into His hands.

2. Send your problems to Him. (vs. 7) If you do not release it, God cannot relieve it. The word translated "casting" literally means "to throw something". God tells us to throw our problems upon Him. That is, push them away from us and let them land into His hands. Make Him responsible for them. That is what prayer is for. "All" means every one of them and every type – personal, family, financial, physical, spiritual, emotional, cares for the present and for the future.

3. Set yourself to resist the devil. (vs. 8-9) When you are under a lot of stress, the enemy of your soul will be nearby, looking for the opportunity to make you sin. He is going to do his best to plant thoughts into your mind to make you worry, complain, become negative, or offended. Refuse his offers. Reject his lies. Remember the promises. Rejoice in the Lord. God is in control.

4. See the Lord working all around you. (vs. 10-11) He did not say that as soon as you place the problem in His hand it would disappear. What He did say is that (a) He is the God of all grace, which means you can count upon Him to give you the unmerited help and ability you need. If His grace does not deliver you from trouble, it will preserve you in trouble; (b) He has called you to His eternal glory in Christ Jesus, which means your tests will end in testimonies, your trials in triumph. He will bring glory out of this for Himself and for you; and (c) He will perfect, strengthen, and settle you. That is His way of saying, don't worry because He is going to get you through this and make you a bigger and better person in the process.

How can I be sure God will work it out for me? "Because," Peter says "He cares for us." In Greek, "cares" is in the present tense, active voice and the indicative mood. This is significant. The present tense means that His caring is continuous, ongoing, and now. The active voice means the Lord Himself is doing it. The indicative mood means that this is a fact! Put it all together and we find that in every circumstance we find ourselves in, Jesus Christ, Himself, is personally, continuously and actively engaged in the ongoing process of providing for us, and this is a fact, not to be doubted!

Let the church say, Amen!

Affirm Today:

"Father when trouble comes I give all of my cares to You. I trust Your care for me. It will always perfect, establish, strengthen, and settle me victoriously."

Additional Scriptures:

1 Peter 5:6-11; Psalm 34:17; 1 John 5:14; Philippians 4:19; 2 Corinthians 9:8

Day 39

Love Not the World

And so it should be for every believer. We are to love God and hate the "world." By the "world" John is not referring to the natural creation, or to people. Creation is good and God loves people. So should we.

The "world" John speaks about is the organized system of evil under the control of the prince of darkness, operated through human beings and demons, which are opposed to God and all those who belong to Him. The world system steals, kills, and destroys. Its ultimate goal is to prevent the will of God from being done on earth.

We are not to love the world. John gives us several reasons why.

1. We are not of this world. We do not belong to it. We are children of God and citizens of heaven.

2. The two loves, love of God and love of the world, are mutually exclusive. They cannot coexist. It's either one or the other.

3. This world is passing away, and the evil thereof, but He who does the will of God abides forever.

Would you board a plane if you knew it was doomed to crash? Would you drive onto a bridge if you knew it would collapse? Would you invest your hard earned savings into a business you knew would fail? Why, then, would you entrust your future to a system doomed to destruction? You shouldn't!

Now, the influence of the world is strong and overcoming it is not simply a matter of will-power. The lust of the flesh, the lust of the eyes, and the pride of life do not yield to human strength alone. Your victory will be obtained through faith, not through will-power.

> *"For whatever is born of God overcomes the world. And this is the victory that has over-come the world—our faith."* (1 John 5:4)

Herein lies the source of your victory – that which God has already accomplished for you and done in you by grace! You see, when you received Jesus as your Lord and Savior, God imparted His Spirit to you. Through your union with the Holy Spirit, you have received a new purpose for living, and a new nature, full of holy desires and a strong love for God. And it is only by means of the new birth and the work of the Spirit in you, energizing your will to do God's will, that victory over the world is experienced.

Child of God, the way to love not the world is to believe God's love for you and all He has wrought for you in Christ Jesus. The more you draw nigh to focus on your union with Jesus and depend on the One who gave His life for you, in order to give His life to you, so that He may live His life through you, the more you will experience His victory as your own. And you will find yourself not loving the world because He who is living in and through you does not love the world.

Affirm Today:

"I am born of God and have overcome the world by my faith in Jesus Christ, the Son of God. He gave His life for me and lives His life through me. In Him I am victorious."

Additional Scriptures:

1 John 2:12-17; 1 John 5:4; Psalm 22:27; Psalm 96:13; Revelation 22:11-12

Day 40

Flourish Like a Palm Tree

In Psalm 92:7, David says, "the wicked spring up like grass," which is here today and gone tomorrow. Then, in verse 12, he says, "the righteous shall flourish like a palm tree." He is making a contrast between the two.

Grasses grow quickly, and die quickly. Expose grasses to extreme heat, and their leaves dry up, wither, and die. That's the way the wicked flourish. They may flourish quickly, but their success will not last. It will all be consumed, either by things in this world, or the judgement of the next.

Not so with the leaves of the palm tree. Even in the desert, in the valleys, or on the mountains, exposed to extreme weather conditions under which other plants cannot live, the leaves of these trees remain green. Their leaves do not dry up, change color, or fall down due to climatic changes around them.

They live very long, hundreds of years, even up to a thousand years, and keep growing and bearing fruit over many years. In fact, the palm tree is one of a few trees that bear more fruit the older it gets. In storms, they bend but they do not break. After the storm they straighten up again, and are actually stronger than they were before the storm.

This is how the righteous flourish. Like the palm, they will continue to grow year after year, under all types of circumstances, reaching higher and higher in their faith, growing continually into the likeness of Christ, expressing more and more of His image.

Like the palm tree, they will endure. The storms of life will not destroy them. They may bend under the weight, but they will not break, and after the storm they are still able to stand upright, walk straight, and keep growing. The heat will not cause them to dry up, nor the cold cause them to freeze up. They flourish under all kinds of conditions.

And they will bear fruit, even in old age.

Child of God, these are God's promises to the righteous. And you are the righteous because Jesus made you righteous. So these are His promises to you. And if you believe, you will see each one of them fulfilled in your life.

Affirm Today:

"I am the righteousness of God in Christ Jesus. Like the palm tree, I will continue to grow stronger, deeper, and higher in every situation. I will endure."

Additional Scriptures:

Psalm 92: 7, 12; Psalm 92:13; Exodus 15:2; John 15:16; Hosea 14:7

Day 41

Say Good-bye to Worry

W hom do you look to for provision, protection and promotion? If you are like most people, you are depending on yourself and because you are, you are under a lot of stress. As a result your life is characterized by worry, fear, and struggle. But there is a better way. It's the way Jesus taught us to live.

> *"Therefore do not worry, saying, 'What shall we eat?' or 'What shall we drink?' or 'What shall we wear?' For after all these things the Gentiles seek. For your heavenly Father knows that you need all these things. But seek first the kingdom of God and His righteousness, and all these things shall be added to you."* (Matthew 6:31-33)

I was blessed with a good earthly father. As his child, I innately knew he would do everything within his power to provide, protect and promote my welfare. I went to bed every night and woke up every day confident that my earthly father was taking care of me and supplying my needs. That's what loving fathers do for their children! And that's why children who have good fathers never worry about shelter or about what they will eat or drink. They know their daddy will provide.

Every good father loves his children and does all he can to ensure they are taken care of. And he will not be satisfied unless his children are doing well. If God is your Heavenly Father, and He is if Jesus is your Savior, then you can be confident He will never be content unless you are doing well. Like any truly good father, your Heavenly Father is taking care of you.

So instead of saying, "How will I make it? I have no one to help me." you should go to bed every night and get up every morning confident your Heavenly Father loves you and that He will take care of you. He knows the things you have need of before you even ask. He even takes care of the birds. Will He not take care of you, His very own child?

Child of God, get to know your Heavenly Father. Accept your Father's love, believe your Father's promise, and tell worry "good-bye". God will provide.

Affirm Today:

"Heavenly Father I am confident that You love me and that You will take care of me. I say good-bye to worry!"

Additional Scriptures:

Matthew 6:31-33; Luke 12:22-28; Ephesians 1:3; Psalm 18:30; Deuteronomy 31:6

Day 42

Divine Protection for Perilous Times

These are perilous times. Bad news is increasing. Evil is abounding. But you do not have to be afraid. Jesus is the Good Shepherd.

During the time of Jesus, a shepherd would lay down his life for his sheep. He loved his sheep so much and took such responsibility for their well-being that he would be willing to pay any price to protect them from evil and supply their needs. Each day, his major concern was the welfare of his sheep, which he placed above his own. And for that reason, exposed as a sheep was to all types of dangers and being so defenseless, having a good shepherd watching over it was absolutely the best thing that could ever happen to a sheep.

Now, listen to these precious words taken from the King James Version of the Bible.

> *"My sheep hear my voice, and I know them, and they follow me: And I give unto them eternal life; and they shall never perish, neither shall any man pluck them out of my hand. My Father, which gave them me, is greater*

*than all; and no man is able to pluck them out
of my Father's hand."* (John 10:27-29, KJV)

He calls you and me, "My sheep." Then, He tells us His Father gave Him to us. He invokes the very personal, loving relationship that existed between a Middle Eastern shepherd and his flock, and applies it to our relationship with Him.

We know His voice and He knows us, and we follow Him – that is His way of saying we belong to Him and He will watch over us forever and take care of us, for He is the Good Shepherd. That is His way of saying He takes personal responsibility for our welfare, and that He will pay any price to ensure we are protected and provided for.

And then He makes a bold promise. His sheep will never perish, be destroyed, or cease to be. Never!

But how can He be so certain? Doesn't He know how evil the world is? Doesn't He know how defenseless we are? Yes, He knows, but He also knows Who He is and what He does to ensure that His sheep is protected and will never perish.

First, He gives to every sheep of His, "eternal life" – a type of life that goes on and on and can never cease to be. It is a life that continues forever without the possibility of ever ending. If you are His sheep, this is the type of indestructible life you have inside of your spirit right now.

Second, He places us in His hands and thus ensures no one would ever be able to separate us from Him to do us harm. And, as if this alone is not enough, His Father, who gave Him to us to be our Shepherd, also has us in His hands. Anyone or thing wanting to harm us must first be able to snatch us out of the hands of both the Father and the Son. That's impossible! They are greater than all.

Child of God, evil will abound more and more. God knows this. He said it would as we approach the end of the Age. But because you are His sheep, you do not need to be afraid. The best thing that could have ever happened to you during these perilous times has happened. God has given you Jesus, the Good Shepherd.

Meditate on Him, not on the evil around you. Then, activate your faith in Him to protect you with your words. Declare daily, "Jesus is my Shepherd. I am safe in His powerful hands. No evil shall befall me." When you focus on Him and confess your faith, He will fill your heart with peace and surround you with His power.

Affirm Today:

"Jesus, I believe You will never leave me or forsake me. I am Your sheep and You know me. You are watching over me and everything that concerns me. Jesus You are my Shepherd. I am safe in Your powerful hands and I am protected."

Additional Scriptures:

John 10:27-29; John 10:28-29; Proverbs 18:10; Psalm 18:2; Psalm 56:3

Day 43

Taking God's Medicine

D o you know that God's Word works like medicine and that it can heal your spirit, soul, and even your body? Unfortunately, if you are a typical Christian, your relationship with the Word is extremely shallow. You spend very little time meditating and renewing your mind in it. And that is a big mistake, because the Word of God contains the power of God that produces health and wholeness. Renewing our minds with the Word is the key to walking in the perfect will of God.

> *"And do not be conformed to this world, but be transformed by the renewing of your mind, that you may prove what is that good and acceptable and perfect will of God."* (Romans 12:2)

Jesus underscored the importance of the Word when He spoke to His disciples and said: *"If you abide in Me and My Words abide in you, you shall ask whatever you will and it shall be given to you"* (John 15:7). Notice that Jesus links the power of answered prayer to a relationship with both Him and His Word.

Here is an illustration to help you understand how hugely critical the Word is to you. Suppose you were extremely ill and decided to seek medical help. You went from doctor to doctor seeking a diagnosis and cure for months to no avail. Then someone recommended you see a particular doctor reputed to be the best in his field. You took the advice. He examined you, diagnosed your condition, and prescribed medication for you to take three times a day the rest of your life. He also required you to see him regularly.

You begin taking the medication and it works! It keeps you alive, as long as you take it daily, as prescribed. Now, tell me, what type of relationship would you have with your doctor? And what type would you have with your medicine?

Because you know your life depends on being under the doctor's care and taking your medication faithfully, you would follow his instructions diligently. You would see him as often as he required, would listen closely to his instruction, and would make taking your medicine three times daily a major priority.

And you would keep your medication near you all the time. The first thing you would do upon waking would be to take your medicine. You would never travel without making sure you had it with you. If you noticed you were without it, you would turn around. And as soon as you noticed your supply was running low, your priority would be to see the doctor for a fresh supply.

Now, this is an apt description of what our relationship with Jesus and the Word of God should be like, if we want to be whole. Our well-being depends on both. Like the doctor, Jesus is our Great Physician. He is the only One who can make us whole. But like the medication, His Words are the means by which He imparts His Life to us and makes us well (John 6:63). They are the means by which we receive His

Life and health into our souls and mortal bodies. Our health and well-being depend on us renewing our minds by hearing and feeding His Words into our hearts and minds consistently.

Listen to the advice of a wise man:

> *"My son, give attention to my words; Incline your ear to my sayings. Do not let them depart from your eyes; Keep them in the midst of your heart; for they are life to those who find them, and health to all their flesh. Keep your heart with all diligence, for out of it spring the issues of life."* (Proverbs 4:20-23)

The word translated "health" in the passage above is also translated "medicine" in some versions. His Words are "medicine to all their flesh."

The wife of a minister was diagnosed with "incurable" cancer and given a few months to live. She decided it was not her time to die and that she would look to God's Word for life. She began meditating on the Word of God regarding healing and feeding on the healing Scriptures day and night. Her symptoms did not immediately get better, but she kept taking God's Word as her medicine, speaking it to God and to herself throughout the day. She kept renewing her mind with the Word, rejecting doubt, until she could "see" herself well, according to the promises. Contrary to the doctors' prognosis, she is alive today, many years later, totally healed, and still serving Jesus! God's Word is medicine.

Child of God, now that you have received Jesus as your personal Savior, you can rest assured that He is always willing to attend to you and minister His healing power to you. But remember, He can only do so if you are willing to take His medicine, the Word, as prescribed. So, cultivate a strong relationship with His Word. Make it your priority to hear His Words concerning healing continually and meditate on them diligently. The more you renew your mind with His Word, the more His Life and medicine can work in you. And the more you will experience His perfect will for your life, and that includes healing you of all your diseases, (1 Peter 2:24, Psalm 103:1-5).

If you are battling sickness of any kind, know it is God's perfect will for you to be whole. As our Redeemer, Jesus took our sicknesses in His body on the cross that we may have a covenant right to enjoy healing and wholeness. So take God's medicine daily and as you do, do not be afraid to declare, "He died young so that I may live long!"

Affirm Today:

"I am renewing my mind by the Word of God and I am being transformed. My mind, body, and circumstances now line up with His Word and manifest His good, acceptable, and perfect will for my life."

Additional Scriptures:

Romans 12:2; John 15:7; 1 Peter 2:24; Psalm 103:1-5; Proverbs 4:20-23

Day 44

Winning Over Discouragement

W hat does a child of God need when facing a mountain of discouragement? When the progress she needs to make in her life is not happening and her best efforts to accomplish a positive goal are going nowhere? When he or she is facing a mountain of discouragement that just won't move? A Word from God, like the one God spoke to Zerubbabel!

After seventy years of captivity in Babylon, about 50,000 Jewish men and women under the leadership of Zerubbabel returned to Jerusalem with a dream of rebuilding the city. Soon work began on the Temple. With much enthusiasm and support, they erected the altar and restored the sacrificial system of worship. Next, they completed the foundation of the Temple and held a powerful thanksgiving service.

Then, trouble hit. Some of the older Jewish people, comparing it to Solomon's Temple, began to criticize the work. And the local residents, Samaritans, decided they would do everything within their power to frustrate Zerubbabel's efforts to rebuild Jerusalem. They hired people to oppose the Jews and wrote letters to the new Persian king accusing the Jews of rebellion. And they succeeded in persuading the king to issue a decree that brought the rebuilding efforts to a halt. For sixteen long years, Zerubbabel's dream remained at a stand-still! A mountain stood before him, one he could not move, no matter how hard he tried.

Then The Lord sent a message to Zerubbabel through the prophet Zechariah:

> *"So he answered and said to me: "This is the word of the Lord to Zerubbabel: 'Not by might nor by power, but by My Spirit,' says the Lord of hosts. 'Who are you, O great mountain? Before Zerubbabel you shall become a plain! And he shall bring forth the capstone with shouts of 'Grace, grace to it!'"*
> (Zechariah 4:6-7)

After sixteen years of being at a standstill, God says to His servant, "I know what you are thinking and how discouraged you feel. But I have come to let you know I will finish this work I started through you. That great mountain that stands in your way will become a plain. Don't worry about its size because you won't have to move it. It is not about your resources or your resoluteness. I will move it by My Spirit. And it will be by My grace, not your works! "

If you are feeling discouraged because time is passing and important, God-given assignments and goals for your life, your family, or your ministry remain unfulfilled, this Word is for you. This is not the time to give up. Rather, this is the time, like Zerubbabel, to hear God say to you, "This mountain shall become a plain, not by your power, but according to My Spirit and by My grace."

Child of God, be encouraged. Our Heavenly Father has entrusted your progress and success into the capable hands of the Holy Spirit. So what He asks of you is not your human strength, just your simple faith. All He needs is for you to believe with your heart that the Holy Spirit, to whom He has given this assignment of completion, is wise enough to know what needs to be done, strong enough to do whatever it takes, and good enough to do so in the way that is best.

So don't give up. Trust! God has promised to finish what He started in you. And the Spirit is well able!

Affirm Today:

"I will not give up. I will trust God. He has promised to finish what He started in me."

Additional Scriptures:

Zechariah 4:6-7; Exodus 14:14; 2 Chronicles 20:17; 2 Samuel 22:33; 1 Corinthians 4:20

Day 45

Stop Trying to Do Things for God

Are you trying hard to work for God? May I suggest you stop? That's right, stop trying so hard to work for God! Now, I know some of you are ready to tie me to the stake and set me on fire for preaching heresy. But before you do, let me explain.

By now we should know the New Covenant is based on grace, not law. What's the difference? Being under law means we do something for God. Being under grace means just the opposite – God does something for us. Under law, God requires things from us to please Him. Under grace, God gives us everything we need Himself. Law demands. Grace supplies.

You see, God is not really interested in us doing things "for" him. After all, what is there that we can do for Him that He cannot do for Himself much better? It's not our works He wants, it's ourselves.

This is the lesson He taught Martha. Jesus was visiting the home of Martha and Mary, two sisters and dear friends of Jesus. During His visit, Martha busied herself in the kitchen preparing food for her special guest, but Mary sat quietly at Jesus' feet, conversing with Him. When Martha complained to Jesus about her sister not helping her in the kitchen to prepare His meal, we would have expected Jesus to tell Mary to go and help her sister, but He does just the opposite. Instead, He tells Martha what would really please Him would be for her to leave the chores and come and join Him and Mary in the living room. He appreciated what she was trying to do for Him, but her work for Him had actually become a distraction from Him.

Martha illustrates what it's like to try to work "for" God. She typifies the person under law, trying to please God and to do her best for God, thinking this is what God expects. She ends up tired. Mary illustrates the person under grace, who has learned to rest in Christ and how to receive from Him. She ends up refreshed.

But what about the work in the kitchen? If Martha joins them in the living room, who will prepare the food and who will clean up afterwards? They will, at the right time, all three of them – Martha, Mary, and Jesus together! And since all three of them would have been well rested and refreshed from their time of relaxation and fellowship in the living room, their work in the kitchen, being a continuation of their fellowship, would be a joy and not a chore!

And this is how God planned it. He does not want us to work "for" Him. That is too hard and beyond our ability. But what He does want is to teach us to rest in Him and then to allow Him to work with us and through us.

Child of God, God has not called you to work for Him in the New Covenant. He's done something much better. He has called you to live "in Christ" by faith so that He can work for you and through you.

Affirm Today:

"Jesus I rest in You and receive from You. I live by grace and not by law."

Additional Scriptures:

Exodus 33:14; Psalm 25:20; Acts 20:32; Psalm 121:1-3; Luke 10:38-42

Day 46

Love and Generosity

Did you know more is said about giving in the New Testament than about prayer, faith, and hell combined? God spends a huge amount of time teaching us to be generous givers. He does this, not to raise cash, but to raise children.

You see, our Father is love and He lives to give. There is nothing He would rather do than share who He is and what He has with anyone who is willing to receive it. And because He is incredibly happy and fulfilled, He wants each of His children to be like Him. "It is more blessed to give than to receive."

Now, one of the reasons God can be so generous is because He is so rich. *"The earth is the LORD's, and all its fullness, the world and those who dwell therein"* (Psalm 24:1). When you have as much as He has, you can afford to give as much as He gives. I am so glad our Father is not only rich in love, He is rich in resources because we are the beneficiaries of His love. He lavishes His great wealth upon His children. *"No good thing will He withhold from those who walk uprightly"* (Psalm 84:11).

But the Father's love and generosity is even more evident by His willingness to give Jesus to us. When He gave Jesus to us, He was not giving out of abundance. He was giving out of scarcity. Out of need. His only Son. What love! What sacrifice!

He calls us to a live a similar life, one of love and generosity.

> *"And as you go, preach, saying, 'The kingdom of heaven is at hand.' Heal the sick, cleanse the lepers, raise the dead, cast out demons. Freely you have received, freely give."* (Matthew 10:7-8)

> *"Give to everyone who asks of you. And from him who takes away your goods do not ask them back. And just as you want men to do to you, you also do to them likewise... But love your enemies, do good, and lend, hoping for nothing in return; and your reward will be great, and you will be sons of the Most High. For He is kind to the unthankful and evil."* (Luke 6:30-36)

Giving generously, with no strings attached, not to get, but to bless – that is how we express ourselves as the sons of God. That is how we demonstrate that we are the Father's children, a chip off the old block, partaking of His divine nature.

Child of God, you have the grace to live this way. You are *"God's workmanship created in Christ Jesus for good works He has ordained for you to walk in"* (Ephesians 2:10). So start acknowledging who you are – the Father's child, what you have – the Father's nature, and what you can do – love like Him. Then begin depending on His Spirit to manifest His generous, loving nature through you. You are your Father's child!

Affirm Today:

"I am my Father's child. His love manifests through me. I joyfully walk in the good works ordained for me and generously give my time, talent and treasure."

Additional Scriptures:

Matthew 10:7-8; Luke 6:30-36; Psalm 24:1; Psalm 84:11; Ephesians 2:10

Day 47

If Money Talks, What Is Yours Saying?

Do you know the Bible talks more about money than about prayer, fasting, heaven, or hell? Knowing how important money is, God spends a huge amount of time teaching us how to view it, obtain it, increase it, and use it. In Matthew 6:21, Jesus says, *"Where your treasure is, there will your heart be also."* Clearly, what we do with money is an accurate indicator of what we feel about God and what we believe God is doing with us.

This is why we find some awesome promises in the Word made to believers who honor God in the use of money.

Paul wrote:

> *"But this I say: He who sows sparingly will also reap sparingly, and he who sows boun-tifully will also reap bountifully. So let each one give as he purposes in his heart, not grudgingly or of necessity; for God loves a cheerful giver. And God is able to make all grace abound toward you, that you, always having all sufficiency in all things, may have an abundance for every good work...Now*

may He who supplies seed to the sower, and bread for food, supply and multiply the seed you have sown and increase the fruits of your righteousness." (2 Corinthians 9:6-10)

Jesus said:

"Give, and it will be given to you: good measure, pressed down, shaken together, and running over will be put into your bosom. For with the same measure that you use, it will be measured back to you." (Luke 6:38)

And we also find some serious warnings.
Paul writes:

"Command those who are rich in this present age not to be haughty, nor to trust in uncertain riches but in the living God, who gives us richly all things to enjoy. Let them do good, that they be rich in good works, ready to give, willing to share, storing up for themselves a good foundation for the time to come, that they may lay hold on eternal life." (1 Timothy 6:17-19)

Jesus said:

"No one can serve two masters; for either he will hate the one and love the other, or else he will be loyal to the one and despise the other. You cannot serve God and mammon." (Matthew 6:24)

It is so important to God that we put Him first in our giving and that we learn to be generous givers. But this is not because He needs our money–He is not hungry, poor, or in debt! No, giving generously is for our benefit.

You see, God wants to be our God and to be the One we depend on to supply all our needs according to His riches in glory by Christ Jesus (Philippians 4:19). He wants to put His grace (unmerited favor, power, ability) to work in our behalf so that we will lack for nothing. In fact, He wants us to have a surplus so that we can be a blessing to others and generous on every occasion.

But what God supplies by grace has to be received through faith. When we are stingy, we show a lack of faith in His sufficiency. But when we honor God by giving to Him the first and best of our finances, and are generous in giving to support His Work and to supply the needs of others, we demonstrate both our faith and love for Him. And because we are operating in faith and not fear, we are able to drink abundantly from the fountain of grace by which every need we have has already been met in Christ Jesus.

Here is a quote from John Piper to help you remember these important truths: "What we do with our money shows what we believe God is doing with us." If we believe our Heavenly Father is caring for us and supplying all our needs according to His riches in glory by Christ Jesus, our wallets and checkbooks will show it. And our hearts will enjoy it!

Since money talks, what is yours saying? I hope it says, God is first in your life, you know He loves you with all His heart, and you truly believe He is taking care of you and meeting all your needs in Christ Jesus.

Affirm Today:

"Freely I have received and freely I give. My God is taking care of me and meeting all my needs in Christ Jesus."

Additional Scriptures:

Philippians 4:19; Luke 6:38; Matthew 6:24; 2 Corinthians, 9:6-10; 1 Timothy 6:17-19; Matthew 6:21

Day 48

Just Killing Time!

On more than one occasion I've asked someone what he was doing and got the response, "Just killing time." Unfortunately, that's what many people do with the time God gives them – they just kill it. But what a sad thing to do with time! When you are killing time, you are not just committing murder. You are committing suicide. You are killing a part of yourself. Time is life.

That is one reason that it's so wrong not to start things on time, and not to keep your appointments because when you cause a person to waste his time you are causing him to waste a portion of his life. A person who does not value his time, does not attach value to life.

This is why the Apostle says to believers in Ephesians 5:15-16, "Do not live as fools, but as wise, redeeming the time, because the days are evil."

It is really unwise to waste time. In fact, it is pure foolishness. Time is too precious to waste.

I do not know what you did with your time this year, but the fact we are here means God has seen fit to give all of us still here a little more time. This is a gift from God. Don't squander it.

Here are two reasons why we cannot afford to squander time:

1. *Because our time on earth is very short.* Many of us have already crossed the half-way mark, the clock is winding down, and the sun is starting to set. The Bible says our life on earth is but a vapor, like rising smoke that vanishes away. When something is in short supply, the value increases. The less you have on hand of a valuable commodity, the more scarce it becomes, the more concerned you are about how you use it.

Job exclaimed that his days were faster than an eagle. And the Psalmist asked God to teach him to number his days so that he could apply his heart to wisdom, (Psalm 90:12). James says as we make plans for tomorrow, we should say, "If God wills."

Time is in short supply. Therefore, it's too valuable to waste. If you do not think this is true, look at yourself in the mirror and that should be enough to let you know you do not have the luxury to waste time.

Our time is so short and the work which we must do is so great that we have no time to spare. Furthermore, we do not even know how short our time is. We do not know how much time we still have left on earth. And that should make every day, every hour God blesses us with on earth more precious.

2. *Because when time is gone, it cannot be recovered.* We all possess many things that we can regain if we part with them. I remember selling my Ford Fairmont Futura when I was in college to a friend. Later, when he wanted to sell it, I bought it back.

I wish I could do this with time. I sometimes look in the mirror and yearn to be 35 again, but that won't happen. Those years have been spent; they are gone forever, and they cannot be recovered. No amount of effort or money can get those years back for me.

So since time is so precious, and to kill time is to kill part of ourselves, since once gone it cannot be recovered, and since the time we have on earth is so short and the work we are called to do so great, what do you plan to do with the time you have left?

"Redeem it," God says. In the Greek, redeeming can mean "to buy up, ransom, or rescue from loss." That means, it is the will of God for you to rescue your time from people, things, habits, entertainment, and all activities that steal your time, that consume it, that squander it. Rescue your time from the time-killers, destiny-destroyers, and purpose-annihilators.

And then what? You are God's workmanship, created in Christ Jesus for good works, which He has ordained for you to walk in, (Ephesians 2:10). Use your rescued time to make the most of every opportunity that God gives you to work on things that you were ordained for – things that really matter to God, that honor Jesus, and bless people!

You get to redeem your time by unloading everyone and everything holding you down, keeping you from running your race and preventing you from pursuing your God-given destiny in Christ and winning your heavenly crown.

Please don't kill time. Use it for the glory of God!

Affirm Today:

"I use my time for the glory of God. I make the most of the opportunities God gives me to work on the things I am ordained for."

Additional Scriptures:

Ephesians 2:10; Psalm 90:12; Ephesians 5:15-16; James 4:13-14; Ecclesiastes 9:12

Day 49

Let It Go

Imagine having to forgive the same person for committing a serious offense against you again and again! Would you think it's fair? Would you find it easy to do so? Probably not.

But this is exactly what Jesus tells us to do. *"If your brother trespasses against you seven times in a day and seven times in a day turns to you saying I repent, you shall forgive him"* (Luke 17:3-4). That does not seem right forgiving a person who keeps hurting me over and over again, especially when his repeated behavior proves he is not really repentant, even though his mouth says so.

When someone does something to hurt you, something on the inside of you may want to hurt him back. Your sense of justice might demand that you do something to get even. You may feel it is just not right to let your offender "get away" with this type of behavior. And as a result you may nurse a grudge for years and become bitter in the process.

But Jesus says you should not handle offenses in that manner. Instead, He insists you choose forgiveness over anger and resentment, even if the offender has not demonstrated genuine remorse. Why?

Because forgiving those who have offended you will set you free! That's right, the principal beneficiary of your decision to forgive will be you. And that is true because the one who suffers most from unforgiveness will always be the one who carries bitterness in his bosom.

Nelson Mandela is famous for choosing to extend forgiveness to those who abused and imprisoned him unjustly. Listen to his words: "Resentment is like drinking poison and waiting for it to kill your enemy."

Author Lewis Smedes writes: "To forgive is to set a prisoner free and discover that the prisoner was you."

When you forgive someone from the heart, you set yourself free from the unhealthy hold they had on you and you take away their power to hurt you.

Forgiveness is hard, but living with a grudge is even harder. Keeping grudges bottled up can be very dangerous, and can hurt you in ways you might have not imagined. When you understand how harmful unforgiveness is to you, you will realize that choosing to release an offender is primarily for your benefit, not theirs.

Let it go.

Affirm Today:

"I accept the freedom true forgiveness brings. I let it go. I choose to forgive and display Your love."

Additional Scriptures:

Psalm 86:5; Matthew, 6:12, 14, 15; Luke 17:3-4; Luke 23:24; Romans 12:19

Day 50

What Forgiveness Is Not

"Do I have to trust him if I forgive him?" This question reflects one of the reasons people find it difficult to forgive. Being asked to let go of resentment and any desire to hurt someone who hurt us is one thing. But being required on top of that to trust that same person again makes it too hard!

The good news is that forgiving a person and trusting him or her are not two sides of the same coin. That means you are not required to trust a person just because you have forgiven him. The two things are related, but very distinct.

Forgiving focuses on an offense committed in the past. It makes it possible for the wounds you carry in your soul as the result of other people's actions to heal. It is a decision you make to set yourself free by setting your offender free. Remember, for you to keep a man down in the gutter you have to be down in the gutter yourself.

Because granting forgiveness to another person is something you are doing for yourself, you can grant it freely and unilaterally. The other person can receive it or reject it, but he or she cannot prevent you from granting it and setting yourself free from the emotional prison you are in.

On the other hand, trust relates to the present and the future. It is the measurement of the dependability, truthfulness, and integrity of a man or woman. Since trust is a measurement, it must be based on verifiable evidence and is dependent on a person's behavior. It, therefore, cannot be subjectively granted. It must be earned.

For this reason, we describe people as "trustworthy." When we do so we are declaring that they have proven themselves worthy of our trust because of their reliable performance in some area. They have earned our confidence by the manner in which they have conducted themselves.

Search the Scriptures and you will find that even though Jesus commands His followers to forgive everybody who sins against them, He never commands them to place their trust in people blindly. On the contrary, He taught them to be gentle as doves, but wise as serpents.

Regarding who to trust, Jesus taught His disciples not to throw pearls before swine. That is, don't entrust something of value to someone who will not take care of it. And in the parable of the talents, He made it clear that a person had to demonstrate he could be trusted with a few talents before he would be trusted with much.

Trusting a person with great responsibilities and with important projects and aspects of our lives, who has not proven himself trustworthy, is not spiritual. It is foolish and irresponsible, and could lead to serious and unnecessary harm to that person and to others.

We have to balance trust with responsibility. The greater the responsibility and the greater the risks, the slower we should be to trust and the higher should be the standard the other person must meet in that area.

For example, a person's word may be all you need to entrust him with your bicycle, but you would be a fool if you did not require a lot more than that person's word before placing yourself and your family in an airplane for him to fly.

So here is my advice: Forgive lavishly and unilaterally. Then give the people you forgive an opportunity to earn your trust, where possible. Don't be unreasonably hard, but don't be naive either. And always balance trust with responsibility.

Hope this helps.

Affirm Today:

"I receive restored relationship with those who have hurt me. I am depending on Your wisdom and trusting Your guidance to manage these relationships."

Additional Scriptures:

Matthew 7:6; Proverbs 8:32; Matthew 10:16; 2 Chronicles 6:30; Psalm 85:5

Day 51

Invest In People

When you mention investing, what comes to mind for most people is investing in real estate or in the stock market. And every day as we watch the news, we hear about how well or how badly the market is doing. People have invested trillions of dollars, much more than we can comprehend, in the stock market. And people who place their money there, do so with the hope that the stocks in their portfolio will do well and that they will make a profit. But, of course, it doesn't always turn out that way!

Now, you may not have much invested in stocks, but you are still an active investor. Every time you say or do something, you are making an investment that will reap dividends either to the glory of God or to the glory of the flesh. Now, what I want to do today is to challenge you to become a wise investor—to invest wisely by investing in what matters most; to invest in people, and not just in houses and lands, in stocks and bonds.

Why people? Let me give you at least one good reason. C.S. Lewis wrote: "There are no ordinary people. You have never talked to a mere mortal. Nations, cultures, arts, civilizations – these are mortal and their life is to ours as the life of a gnat. But it is immortals, whom we joke with, work with, marry; snub, and exploit – immortal horrors or everlasting splendors." Every person you have ever met is immortal and will live forever as either an immortal horror in hell or an everlasting splendor in heaven. Let that sink in for a moment. Invest in people because they are the only thing immortal you can invest in.

When I look back on my life, I can clearly see that there were people who invested heavily in me. My number 1 investor was my mother. She left this world for heaven. I miss her, but my mother lives on in me. By her love, her sacrifices, her faith and her prayers, she invested in me, shared her life with me, and made me who I am today. She planted seeds that will continue to bear fruit for many years to come.

My mother was my number 1 investor, but she was not the only person who poured into my life wisdom, knowledge, time and resources, without which I would not be who I am today. I remember my third grade teacher, Mrs. Plaska, who by her words made me feel at that young age that I was special and that I could do great things with my life. I remember Pastor Conley, a Baptist pastor, who may not have been the greatest preacher, but who loved me and gave me an opportunity when I was a student to work with him. He invested in me in so many ways, including letting me borrow his Cadillac to take my new bride on her honeymoon because I was too poor to afford to rent a car! I remember my pastor, Bishop Laurore, who affirmed me in my call, believed in me, and ordained me to the ministry. And of course, Oral Roberts, who built a university on faith, saw my potential and decided to give me a scholarship to attend his school. All of these people invested in me and have a share in making me who I am today.

When we make investing in people our way of life, we are being like the Son of God. On one occasion, Jesus said, *"If I be lifted up, I will draw all men unto me"* (John 12:32). This expresses a philosophy of life that Jesus practiced. He knew that He would be lifted up and as a result of being lifted up would be in a position of great authority and power. Therefore, He made it His goal not to use that authority and power for the benefit of Himself alone. He made the quality decision that He would use His position to lift others up to a new position as well. When you make it your philosophy of life to invest in others, to lift other people up, you are living like Jesus lived. And when you live like Jesus did, you extend your influence to generations unborn.

"Now", someone might ask, "what do I have that others need? I am not highly educated, I am not wealthy, and I do not have any special gifts." Sure, if God has blessed you with education and wealth you should use them to bless others, but the truth is, investing in other people does not require any of those things. Remember, the widow of Zarephath. What did she have? A little flour and a jar of oil! She could have kept it for herself and her son thinking that it was so little and that it would make no difference. But she didn't. Instead, she decided to share it with Elijah; to invest in him. It was a sacrifice, but it was one well worth it. Not only did she feed the prophet, she ended up feeding herself and her son as the result. And this is a truth you need to know about investing in other people. When you add value to others, you add even more value to yourself. When you help others, you help your-self and you create a legacy from which even your children will benefit.

Don't live a selfish life. Invest in what matters. And remember, at the end of your life, when you meet God, the only thing that will matter is, did you love Jesus and did you invest in people.

Affirm Today:

"Lord, show me how to extend myself in new ways that bless people and honor You."

Additional Scriptures:

John 12:32; 1 Kings 17:13-16; Deuteronomy 32-9; Matthew 10:8; Mark 10:45

Day 52

Is God For You?

To be for a person is to be in support of and in favor of that person. And to favor a person is to give that person preferential treatment over others. Stop and think about the implications.

The Word says, God is for us. This means, the Almighty, the most powerful Person in the universe, will support us and give us preferential treatment over others. He will make our interest and well-being His top priority in every situation every day.

How can we be absolutely certain this is the case? Firstly, because He said so. Secondly, because of what He did. He spared not His own Son, but delivered Him over for us all.

If anyone questions if God is for us, His willingness to let His Son die so we may live should settle all doubts. How could He make such a sacrifice and not be completely devoted to us and committed to our well-being? Impossible!

And since this is the case, the text asks, who can be against us? That is, who would dare be against someone God is for? No one with any sense!

Child of God, if because He is for you, God spared not His own Son, you can be certain that because He is for you, He will bless you with all things you will ever need to make your life complete. And He will do so freely; that is, without any limitations on Him and without any charge to you.

What else would you expect from such a God!

Affirm Today:

"My God is for me. I am preferred. Blessed without limitation and without charge."

Additional Scriptures:

1 Corinthians 15:57; 1 John 5:4; Romans 8:31-32; Ephesians 3:20; Zechariah 4:6

Day 53

Blessing You Is God's Idea

D o you ever need a favor from someone but you are afraid to ask because you are not sure how he or she will respond? It can be hard to ask for help when you are uncertain about the outcome. But when it comes to God, you can be sure even before you ask that He is eager to help you in times of need.

You see, God made the decision to bless you with every blessing long before He created you. He decided to hear your prayers and shower you with supernatural provisions before you were born. While you were still in your sins, He purposed in His heart to forgive you of every one of them and treat you as a favored son forever.

> *"But God commended His love toward us in that while we were yet sinners Christ died for us."* (Romans 5:8)

> *"If God spared not His Son but delivered Him up for us all, how shall He not now with Him freely give us all things?"* (Romans 8:32)

> *"But of Him are we in Christ who has been made unto us wisdom, righteousness, sanctification and redemption."* (1 Corinthians 1:30)

Numerous Biblical passages like these assure us of God's love. What they demonstrate is that God's desire to bless us is even stronger than our desire to be blessed. What they prove is we do not need to persuade God to do us good because the idea of doing us good entered His mind before it entered ours. God does not need to be persuaded to bless us!

Then who needs to be persuaded? We do! It is we who need to be persuaded that God is committed to freely giving us all things we need for life and godliness. It is we who need to know beyond all doubt that we are blessed and highly favored with every spiritual blessing in Christ Jesus. And it is we who need to be convinced that no good thing will He withhold from us!

Child of God, get persuaded! Feed on the Word of Grace continually. Do so devotedly. And you will discover that the more persuaded you are, the more blessed you will be.

So, the next time you are struggling with believing God for a blessing, remember the thought of blessing you entered His mind long before it entered yours.

Affirm Today:

"I am blessed and highly favored with every spiritual blessing in Christ Jesus. No good thing will You withhold from me."

Additional Scriptures:

1 Corinthians 1:30; Romans 8:32; Romans 5:8; 2 Peter 1:3; Ephesians 1:3

Day 54

God Freely Gives to You All Things

It's unfortunate that so many Christians have not grasped the extent of the Father's love and how eager He is to meet their needs. They beg, they cry, they sacrifice, all in an effort to "get" God to hear their prayers. To persuade Him to meet their needs. But is any of this necessary?

Consider the following verses:

> *"Do not fear, little flock, for it is your Father's good pleasure to give you the kingdom."* (Luke 12:32)

> *"Look at the birds of the air, for they neither sow nor reap nor gather into barns; yet your heavenly Father feeds them. Are you not of more value than they?"* (Matthew 6:26)

> *"What then shall we say to these things? If God is for us, who can be against us? He who did not spare His own Son, but delivered Him up for us all, how shall He not with Him also freely give us all things?"* (Romans 8:31-32)

169

God's love for you is astonishing. And because of His great love for you, He will withhold no good thing from you. Neither do you need to persuade Him with your tears and good works to convince Him to meet your needs.

In fact, if you look closely at Romans 8:31-32, you will discover an amazing truth. God did not spare His own Son, but delivered Him up for you. And when did He do this? When you were an unholy, rebellious sinner!

But look again. What else does it say? God freely gives you all things. All things you need for life and godliness, God freely – with absolutely no cost to you, gives to you! And when did He do so? "With Jesus," two-thousand years ago! God took care of all your needs when He delivered up Jesus for you two-thousand years ago.

Child of God, never doubt your Heavenly Father's love for you, how eager He is to help you, and His commitment to seeing to it that your needs are met. There is no need to beg for what He already has given you. Instead of worrying, meditate on His Word, believe His promises, give thanks, and rest in His love.

Affirm Today:

"I gladly release doubt and accept faith in God and His Word as the firm foundation of my life. His Word freely gives me all things. Blessings overflow in my life."

Additional Scriptures:

Romans 8:31-32; Psalm 8:6; Psalm 57:2; Luke 12:32; Matthew 6:26

Day 55

Do You Know The Answer to This Question?

Was it Mark Twain who said the two most important days in life are the day you were born and the day you discover why? You undoubtedly know the day you were born, but do you know why? Don't let this important question go unanswered.

Jesus was only 12 years old when He said to His earthy parents: *"Why did you seek Me? Did you not know that I must be about My Father's business"* (Luke 2:49)? At this very young age, He already knew who He was and why He was born. He was God's Son and He was born to conduct Heaven's business on earth.

We know that doing the Father's business took Jesus to different towns and villages in Israel *"doing good and healing all those who were oppressed of the devil"* (Acts 10:38). Doing the Father's business eventually took Him to the cross, the grave, the resurrection, and the throne. And, it is to do the Father's business that He will come again with a shout, with the voice of an archangel, and every eye will see Him, and every knee will bow before Him, and confess that He is Lord of lords. All of this because He was able to say at age 12, I was born to do the Father's business, and the Father's business I will do.

Now, how old are you? Probably older than 12! Have you determined why you were born yet? The sooner you can answer the "why", the more quickly you will know the "how".

But let me help you. Let me get you started in the right direction. You too are God's child and just like Jesus, you were placed on earth to conduct Heaven's business. So, this is where to begin, with what you already know. Start saying daily, "I am God's child and I am about my Father's business." He will fill in the details.

Affirm Today:

"I am God's child and I am about my Father's business. I am ready for His plan for my life."

Additional Scriptures:

Ephesians 1:11; Romans 8:30; Ephesians 2:10; Luke 2:49; Isaiah 41:9

Is It Time To Leave Your Nest?

Before a baby eagle is hatched, its nest is prepared to provide a safe, comfortable place for it to be born, to grow, and be protected, because at that stage in its development, that is what it needs. A nice, warm, comfortable place. At that stage, it has nothing to do but to sleep, eat, and grow.

And that baby loves it! What a way to live! What a place to be! How comfortable, how convenient! Why mess with such a wonderful arrangement?

But things are destined to change. As it develops and starts to grow feathers, the eaglet notices that the nest is changing under it. Thorns start to appear in the nest. And now the nest that once brought it nothing but pleasure is beginning to be irritating, even painful at times.

What is happening? Mother eagle is stirring up the nest. She is removing the straws that once covered the thorns and made the nest comfortable for her baby. On purpose, she is destroying the nest she built. It may seem strange, and even mean of her to do so, but this is really an act of love.

Consider the implications. Her baby is an eagle. Her baby has wings. Those wings now have feathers. Her baby can fly. But her baby does not know this. And besides, her baby is so comfortable being in the nest that unless some-thing happens to motivate it to leave the nest, it will remain in the nest all its life and die there.

What a tragedy, to be an eagle, to have eagle genes, eagle vision, eagle speed, eagle strength, eagle wings and die in the nest, without ever flying! No eagle should die in the nest. No eagle should die without ever flying.

But an even greater tragedy is to be a child of God, a partaker of the divine nature, one spirit with Christ, and live like a mere man! To be born of God and never know experientially what it is like to manifest the divine nature– to talk, walk, and love like God Himself. No child of God should die in the nest. No child of God should die without soaring like an eagle.

> *"Even the youths shall faint and be weary, And the young men shall utterly fall, But those who wait on the LORD Shall renew their strength; They shall mount up with wings like eagles, They shall run and not be weary, They shall walk and not faint."*
> (Isaiah 40:30 31)

Child of God, is it time to leave your nest? Are you willing to leave your comfort zone to fulfill your high calling in Christ? You have supernatural genes and wings of faith. You can soar! So, what are you waiting for to stretch your wings of faith and let the wind of His Spirit take you higher than you ever thought possible?

Let the flying begin!

Affirm Today:

"I am ready to leave the nest of my comfort zone and embrace new possibilities. I am fulfilling my calling certain of success. Like the eagle I will rise."

Additional Scriptures:

Daniel 11:32; Jeremiah 27:5; Philippians 4:13; Ephesians 1:18-19; Isaiah 40:30-31

Day 57

Who's Afraid of the Devil?

When you hear some people talk, you would think the devil is more powerful than God! They are afraid of him. In their minds, he is omnipresent and omnipotent and the epitome of evil; someone they are to run from as fast as they can or else he will destroy them. But, are these things true?

The only thing true is that he is the epitome of evil. Everything else is a lie he has fabricated about himself to keep people from knowing his true condition. His only hope is that you will not discover what Jesus did to him. So let me expose him for the liar he is.

Speaking of what Jesus did to Satan's kingdom on the cross in Colossians 2:15, the Message Bible reads: *"He stripped all the spiritual tyrants in the universe of their sham authority at the Cross and marched them naked through the streets"* (Colossians 2:15, MSG). Jesus took away all his authority and power on the cross.

Recounting what happened after the disciples returned from a successful time of ministry in Luke 10:17-20, the New King James Bible reads:

"Then the seventy returned with joy, saying, 'Lord, even the demons are subject to us in Your name.' And He said to them, 'I saw Satan fall like lightning from heaven.'"

Satan lost. Jesus won and then gave us power over all devils.

Speaking of our permanent position of victory over the devil in 1 John 4:4, the NKJV reads: *"You are of God, little children, and have overcome them, because He who is in you is greater than he who is in the world."* The devil is no match for the Greater One who is in us. No match!

Is the devil still active and able to cause harm? Yes, but since he has been stripped of all his own authority and power, he has to depend upon the power we give him to do his dastardly deeds. Men must empower him with their words and deeds, or he is powerless.

Who's afraid of the devil? Not I, and neither should you.

Affirm Today:

"I stand on the truth of God's Word and who I am in Jesus Christ. I am fearless and victorious. I do not run from the devil. The devil runs from me."

Additional Scriptures:

Luke 10:17-20; 1 John 4:4; James 4:7; Isaiah 41:10; Colossians 2:15

Day 58

What's Before You, Blessings or Curses?

When you look into your future, what do you see? Blessings or curses? I remember a song we sang decades ago, "I Have Decided to Follow Jesus." The lyrics of one of its verses were, "The Cross before me, the world behind me...no turning back." It is a powerful song of consecration. It reminds us of our decision to stop living for self and to start living for Christ. It enjoins us to keep our eyes on the Cross.

But we should not lose sight of the fact that the Cross upon which Jesus died is actually behind us. That's right! The Lamb of God was slain before the foundation of the world and it was nearly two-thousand years ago that Jesus was crucified for us.

Now, this is hugely important. Why? Because it was on the Cross that Jesus broke the power of sin and delivered us from sin's penalty. It was on the Cross that He brought an end to the law of sin and death, and where the reign of grace began. It was at the cross that the curse ceased and undeserved blessings and favor began. At the cross heavenly demands gave way to divine supply.

Think about this for a moment. If the Cross is where God overcomes everything for you and the Cross is behind you, then sin and judgment, sickness and poverty, fear and failure are permanently behind you. They were all overcome for you at the Cross.

Now, because Jesus overcame every curse for you at the Cross, and solved every problem there, you won't need to overcome them in your strength. You simply need to receive your victory by faith. The way you do this is to look back at the Cross and see Jesus conquering every problem there for you. And then, while fixing your eyes on the Cross, instead of confessing fear, keep boldly declaring your faith in Jesus' finished work.

So, when you look at the Cross today, it should be like looking in the rear view mirror of a rapidly moving vehicle and seeing, not what is coming your way, but all those curses Jesus overcame for you moving further and further away from you. You are leaving them behind, permanently, on the Cross. Child of God, start filling your heart with great expectations by boldly declaring every day, "The curse is behind me; God's blessings are before me. No turning back. No turning back."

Affirm Today:

"The curse is behind me; God's blessings are before me. No turning back. No turning back."

Additional Scriptures:

1 Corinthians 15:57; 1 John 5:4; Psalm 105:24; Psalm 111:5; Galatians 6:14

Day 59

Indestructible

"There are those who plotted against you and don't know how you survived. And those who tried to bury you who did not know you were a seed. You popped up and started growing." I saw this statement on the internet recently and wanted to share it with you because it is such a powerful way to convey the truth about Jesus' life in you. It makes you indestructible, victorious, and more than a conqueror.

In this world, you will experience troubles – all types. That is no secret. Jesus warned us to anticipate them. He also assured us of victory. But, we need to believe and boldly declare what God has said concerning us.

That is what Jesus did as He faced the cross. In Luke 24, we see that He acknowledged the trouble He was going to face, but instead of giving in to doubt and fear, He made sure to boldly confess the victory His Father had promised Him. Jesus declared, *"The Son of Man must be delivered into the hands of sinful men, and be crucified, and the third day rise again"* (Luke 24:7).

Jesus knew He was the Seed and being buried by trouble would only cause Him to "pop up and start growing." But He made sure to confess His faith in that blessed reality. The rest is history. On the third day He arose.

Here is one of many powerful promises for you to claim:

> *"Now thanks be to God who always leads us in triumph in Christ, and through us diffuses the fragrance of His knowledge in every place."*
> (2 Corinthians 2:14)

Child of God, when He promises always to lead you in triumph, God means exactly what He says. He will cause you to triumph always, regardless of the circumstances. But, you need to believe this promise to experience it personally. That means your attitude should always be one of victory and instead of going around confessing fear and defeat, you should be declaring boldly that God always causes you to triumph in Christ Jesus and that it is impossible for your story to ever end in defeat.

The Bible declares that as Jesus is, so are we in this world. Jesus Himself declared that because He lives, we will live also. Romans 8:37 proclaims we are more than conquerors in Christ Jesus. Now, all this leads to one inescapable conclusion: When trouble tries to bury you, you will "pop up and start growing." Indestructible.

Affirm Today:

"I am indestructible, an overcomer rooted and confidently growing in the love of God. My triumph is in Jesus Christ. My story is destined for victory."

Additional Scriptures:

1 Corinthians 2:14; Romans 8:37; 2 Corinthians 5:7; Ephesians 2:4-6; Luke 24:7

Day 60

Desiring to Win

Paul had a drive to win.

> *"Brethren, I do not count myself to have appre-*
> *hended; but one thing I do, forgetting those*
> *things which are behind me and reaching for-*
> *ward to those things which are ahead, I press*
> *toward the goal for the prize of the upward*
> *call of God in Christ Jesus."* (Philippians
> 3:13-14)

He said, "I forget the things that are behind; I am straining; I am like a runner; I am pressing because I intend to win." When you are focused on one thing, you have a drive to win in life. You refuse to come to the end of your life as a failure. At the end of your life, you want to be able to say, I fought the good fight. I finished my course. I kept the faith. Now there awaits for me in heaven a crown of righteousness. I win! Every man and woman who is focused on knowing Christ and making Him known is driven by an insatiable desire to win in life. I've seen people lose basketball games and get depressed. How much more should we be concerned that we win this Christian race! How much more should we be driven by a desire to win in life! We must not be like the man in Luke 12:16-21:

> *Then he spoke a parable to them, saying: "The ground of a certain rich man yielded plenti-fully. And he thought within himself, saying, 'what shall I do, since I have no room to store my crops? So he said, I will do this: I will pull down my barns and build greater, and there I will store all my crops and my goods. And I will say to my soul, "Soul, you have many goods laid up for many years; take your ease: eat, drink, and be merry."' But God said to him, 'fool! This night your soul will be required of you; then whose will those be which you have provided?' "So is he who lays up treasure for himself, and is not rich towards God."*

God called him a fool, for he had spent all his life acquiring only material things, pursuing only material dreams, and set-ting only earthly goals. Nothing that he had done had eternal value. God looked at him and said, "fool!"

May none of you hear Jesus say, "Fool! You had such an opportunity, but you wouldn't open your eyes; you refused to open your ears; you refused to open you heart; you refused to hear My voice. When the Word of God was spoken, you hard-ened your heart. I intended for you to be a winner. I intended for you to come at the end of your life as more than a con-queror. I intended for you to be crowned with glory, but you spent 70 years chasing empty dreams, meaningless things."

Today, if you hear God saying "do one thing- live to know My Son and make him known," don't harden your heart. Open your heart, and say, Yes, God!

Affirm Today:

"I forget what is behind me and press forward to what is ahead. I am a winner living to know Jesus and make Him known."

Additional Scriptures:

Philippians 3:13-14; Luke 12:16-21; Isaiah 49:4; Colossians 3:23-24; 2 Timothy 1:9

Day 61

Are the Odds Against You?

What should you do if the odds against you accomplishing an important goal are 450 to 1? Would that cause you to faint? Do you have the faith required to proceed?

In Judges 6:15, when Israel cried out to the Lord to deliver them from the Midianites, He gave Gideon the impossible assignment of leading Israel into battle. But Gideon protested.

> *"Who am I? I am the least in my family, my family is the least in my clan, my clan is the least in my tribe, and my tribe is the least in Israel."*

Gideon was totally inadequate for this role. He was a farmer with absolutely no military experience. The Midianites were a far superior army. And they outnumbered Israel four to one.

But the Lord did a strange thing. As if the odds were not bad enough, He reduced Gideon's small army even further to only 300 men. The Midianites had an army of 140,000! Talking about being outnumbered; for every one of Gideon's men, there were now more than 450 heavily armed Midianite soldiers.

"Then the Lord said to Gideon, 'By the three hundred men who lapped I will save you, and deliver the Midianites into your hand.'"
(Judges 7:7)

This was humanly impossible, but God did exactly what He said. We read in chapter 8:28:

"Thus Midian was subdued before the children of Israel, so that they lifted their heads no more. And the country was quiet for forty years in the days of Gideon."

Child of God, have you received a negative report from your doctor? Have you lost your job and can't see how you will make it financially? Do you have things to do that are far beyond your natural ability? Are you tempted to give in to despair and hopelessness?

Before you do, think of Gideon. The truth is, when God is on your side, the odds can never be against you. When God is for you, the odds are always in your favor! God plus you equals success. God plus you equals victory.

Affirm Today:

"Lord with You I can do anything. You are unlimited and all powerful. I steadfastly reject any roadblock in my path and confidently move forward in victory. You are my sword, my shield and my strong tower. I am brave and victorious because of You. I know in Christ I win."

Additional Scriptures:

Jeremiah 32:17; Matthew 19:26; Judges 6:15; Judges 7:7; Judges 8:28

Day 62

Don't Run!

N otice how Peter described the devil. He used the personal possessive adjective, *your*. This means Satan is not just "the" enemy; he is "your" personal enemy. And you are his personal target.

You may think that you are insignificant; that because you are not a bishop, or Reverend So and So, Satan does not know you or care about you. But the truth is, Satan understands the potential of every believer and how much God is capable of accomplishing through you because you are in Christ Jesus; of how many lives Christ can impact and influence and rescue through you. He knows how dangerous you are to him and what a treasure you are to God.

And for this reason, he is "roaming about like a roaring lion seeking whom he may devour." Now, this ought not to frighten you, but inform you of how he operates. A lion that roars is a lion that does not have much confidence and wants to see whether a potential prey will run or resist. Satan makes a lot of noise, he "roars," to see if he can frighten you. He knows he can only succeed against those who are afraid of him.

So how should you deal with him?

"But he gives more grace. Therefore he says, God resists the proud, but gives grace unto the humble. Submit yourselves, therefore, to God. Resist the devil, and he will flee from you." (James 4:6-7)

On several occasions, Satan sent a messenger to trouble the Apostle Paul. Three times Paul prayed asking God to get rid of this demonic messenger. And God answered Paul with these words: *"My grace is sufficient for you, for my strength is made perfect in weakness"* (1 Corinthians 12:9).

Child of God, when Satan roars, don't run. Instead, simply resist him. How? By turning to God in humility, every time you hear the roar, and relying on His grace – unmerited favor and undeserved ability.

Indeed, His grace is sufficient. Sufficient to make the enemy flee, every time. Hallelujah!

Affirm Today:

"God's strength is made perfect in my weakness. I resist the devil and he runs from me."

Additional Scriptures:

James 4:6-7; 1 Corinthians 12:9; 1 John 4:4; Revelation 12:11; 1 Peter 5:8

Day 63

Is Jesus Having an Affair?

A dultery is a sin. It occurs when a married person develops an intimate relationship with someone other than his or her spouse. The Law forbids it. God frowns on it. Jesus is accused of it. Is He guilty?

Who would dare accuse Jesus of any sin, especially this kind? Evil, sacrilegious men – they have made movies and written books suggesting this nonsense. It's shocking, but not surprising, coming from such men. But, they are not the only ones accusing Jesus of sin. Sadly, without knowing what they are doing, many believers in Jesus are doing the same thing.

Let's take a quick look at Scripture. Pay particular attention to the last verse in the passage below, Romans 7:4. Notice what is said about our relationship to the Law and what had to happen in order for us to be joined or married to Christ spiritually.

> *"Or do you not know, brethren (for I am speaking to those who know the law), that the law has jurisdiction over a person as long as he lives? For the married woman is bound by law to her husband while he is living; but if*

*her husband dies, she is released from the law
concerning the husband. So then, if while her
husband is living she is joined to another man,
she shall be called an adulteress; but if her
husband dies, she is free from the law, so that
she is not an adulteress though she is joined
to another man. Therefore, my brethren, you
also were made to die to the Law through the
body of Christ, so that you might be joined to
another, to Him who was raised from the dead,
in order that we might bear fruit for God."*
(Romans 7:1-4, NASB)

This passage reveals that we were once "married" to the
Law legally in an exclusive spiritual union. Unfortunately,
even though the Law was good, because of the weaknesses of
our flesh, the relationship between the Law and us produced
nothing but "fruit for death."

*"For while we were in the flesh, the sinful pas-
sions, which were aroused by the Law, were at
work in the members of our body to bear fruit
for death."* (Romans 7:5, NASB)

Something needed to change, or we would continue to
produce nothing but sin. We needed to be joined to Someone
other than the law, to a Person potent enough to overcome the
flesh in order to produce fruit for God through us. We needed
to be married to Christ to produce the fruit of holiness.

But this marriage to Christ could not occur until our relationship with the Law was permanently and totally dissolved.
Otherwise, He would be guilty of adultery. The dissolution
took place on Calvary. That is where our marriage to the
Law ended, and when our marriage to Christ began. And
now, being joined to Christ legally, He is able to bear fruit

unto God through us. He places His life in our spirits, and our spirits manifest His fruit – His holiness, effortlessly, as we behold Him and gaze upon His loveliness daily.

Child of God, if you are still trying to have a relationship with the Law, trying to produce fruit unto God through self-effort and law-keeping, then without knowing it, you are committing spiritual adultery. And sadly, you are implicating Jesus in an "affair" since He is interested in producing fruit unto God through you.

You were made to die to the Law through the body of Christ. So stop trying to resurrect this relationship. It can only produce fruit for death – guilt, condemnation, and more sin. Instead, receive the gift of righteousness and focus on intimacy with Jesus. It is your intimate relationship with Jesus, your exclusive focus on His love and grace, which will give life to you. Never forget, you are already joined to Him who was raised from the dead, and through this union that is already in existence, trust Jesus to manifest fruit through you. Not by your power, but by His Spirit!

Affirm Today:

"I receive Your gift of righteousness Jesus and focus on our intimate relationship which gives me life. I trust You to manifest fruit through me by Your Spirit."

Additional Scriptures:

Zechariah 4:6; John 15:4-5; John 15:8; John 15:16; Romans 7:1-5

Day 64

Will Grace Cause You to Sin?

Have you ever heard some well-meaning Christian say that too much of grace will cause people to sin? Probably. That warning, unfortunately, accomplishes just the opposite of what is intended. Inadvertently, it is actually encouraging believers to take their eyes off of Jesus to some degree (however small), in order to engage the flesh in their battle to overcome the flesh. Now that is a sure recipe for spiritual failure!

> *"For the mind set on the flesh is death, but the mind set on the Spirit is life and peace, because the mind set on the flesh is hostile toward God; for it does not subject itself to the law of God, for it is not even able to do so, and those who are in the flesh cannot please God."* (Romans 8:6-7)

What does having a "mind set on the flesh" mean? Contrary to what many think, when Paul speaks of a "mind set on the flesh," he is not speaking only of a mind set on immoral things. He is, in fact, principally speaking of a person who is trying to serve God with the ability of the flesh. He has in mind both the notorious sinner and the highly religious person who is trying to fix the flesh with the flesh. Such a person cannot please God.

What does such a person need? Grace added upon grace and more grace on top of that! Grace is the solution, not the problem. Instead of causing people to sin, grace teaches believers to say no to ungodliness. And, even more importantly, empowers them not to sin.

> *"For the grace of God that brings salvation has appeared to all men, teaching us that, denying ungodliness and worldly lusts, we should live soberly, righteously, and godly in the present age, looking for the blessed hope and glorious appearing of our great God and Savior Jesus Christ, who gave Himself for us, that He might redeem us from every lawless deed and purify for Himself His own special people, zealous for good works."* (Titus 2:11-14)

Preaching grace is telling men to look to Jesus and His finished work for everything. It is proclaiming Jesus as the answer to every question and the solution to every problem. It is refusing to put any confidence in the ability of the flesh. It is denying that any good thing can be produced by the flesh, especially the religious flesh. It is telling men to look to Jesus and what He did for them alone; to never take their eyes off Him, regardless of outward circumstances and failures. It is He who purifies us for Himself and makes us zealous for good works.

Child of God, can it ever be true that looking totally and always unto Jesus alone will cause you to sin? Grace does not cause you to sin. It places your eyes on Jesus, allowing Him to work in you both to will and do His good pleasure.

Affirm Today:

"Jesus, I praise You that my eyes are on You and Your grace is teaching me to say no to sin. I refuse to put any confidence in my flesh. Thank you for enabling me to live soberly, righteously and godly in this present evil age."

Additional Scriptures:

Romans 8:6-7; Romans 8:12-13; Romans 8:14; Act 20:32; Titus 2:11-14

Day 65

Standing

D o you know the difference between your standing and your state? If you don't, you need to. Knowing the difference is critical to your Christian walk and growth. So pay attention!

Your standing is your position in heaven before God. It is determined by how God sees you.

> *"Blessed be the God and Father of our Lord Jesus Christ, who hath blessed us with all spiritual blessings in heavenly places in Christ: According as he hath chosen us in him before the foundation of the world, that we should be holy and without blame before him in love."* (Ephesians 1:3-4, KJV)

> *"For He made Him who knew no sin to be sin for us, that we might become the righteousness of God in Him."* (2 Corinthians 5:21)

Your standing is eternal and unchangeable. It is a gift of grace provided to all who look to Jesus for salvation and not to themselves. As long as you are in Christ, this is how God sees you. Your standing is not based on your behavior. That means your behavior does not change your standing. It is solely a result of God's love and grace.

Your state, however, is your condition on earth before men. It is determined by how you see God.

> *"By faith he forsook Egypt, not fearing the wrath of the king; for he endured as seeing Him who is invisible."* (Hebrews 11:27)

> *"For we walk by faith, not by sight."* (2 Corinthians 5:7)

Your state is temporal and changeable. It is a function of your circumstances and your faith. And your faith is a function of how you see God at any moment.

As long as you are in this body and on this earth, your state will be affected by your faith. See God as He is, in whatever circumstance you find yourself, and you will experience joy and peace. Fail to see Him, or see Him as He is not, and you will experience fear and condemnation.

Circumstances change. And often not in the way we would choose. In an instant, you can go from having the time of your life to being in the midst of the greatest battle you ever faced. It only takes one temptation, one person, one trial, for your feelings and behavior to go south. I know what I am talking about. I've been there.

Circumstances change, but your standing does not. The key to victorious living, therefore, is to remember that your standing before God is determined by how God has chosen to see you in Jesus; and that God does not permit your standing before Him in heaven to be affected by your state before men on earth. In Jesus, you are forever the righteousness of

God in Christ. In Jesus, you are always holy and blameless in God's sight.

So, when your earthly condition is out of alignment with your heavenly position, what should you do? Take your eyes off your temporal state and get them focused on your eternal standing.

> *"For our light affliction, which is but for a moment, is working for us a far more exceeding and eternal weight of glory, while we do not look at the things which are seen, but at the things which are not seen. For the things which are seen are temporary, but the things which are not seen are eternal."* (2 Corinthians 4:17-18)

> *"If then you were raised with Christ, seek those things which are above, where Christ is, sitting at the right hand of God. Set your mind on things above, not on things on the earth. For you died, and your life is hidden with Christ in God. When Christ who is our life appears, then you also will appear with Him in glory."* (Colossians 3:1-4)

Child of God, this is what it means to walk by faith and not by sight. Start focusing on your standing and not on your state. Start relying on your heavenly position and stop dwelling on your earthly condition. Then joy and peace will be yours, regardless of the circumstance. Not sometimes. Always.

Affirm Today:

"Thank you Father, I am blessed with all spiritual bless-ings in heavenly places in Christ. I am righteous, chosen by God, assured that my standing is eternal and unchangeable. Purposefully I choose to focus on my standing. Daily I rejoice as my circumstances change because I am practicing walking by faith and not by sight."

Additional Scriptures:

2 Corinthians 5:21; Hebrews 11:27; 2 Corinthians 4:17-18; Colossians 3:1-4; Ephesians 1:3-4; 2 Corinthians 5:7

Day 66

Are You Struggling With Being Faithful?

"*Go tell my disciples, and Peter, I am risen*" (Mark 16:7). He singles Peter out; makes special mention of him; calls him by name. Why? Peter had just denied Him three times, was feeling utterly worthless, completely rejected, a total failure. Peter had given up on himself. Jesus would never give up on him.

Do you sometimes feel like a failure, that God must be angry with you and probably wants to have nothing to do with you again because you let Him down? Do you condemn yourself and feel useless and unworthy because you have not been faithful? Then you understand exactly what Peter was thinking and feeling, and why Jesus gave him such special attention.

Child of God, God does not love you because you are good. He makes you good because He loves you. That's why your failures do not disqualify you. They do not cause Jesus to reject you. In fact, if they do anything at all, they cause Him to grieve for you and draw closer to you to bring you out of the situation you've placed yourself in.

That is what He did for Peter. Instead of condemning him for his failure, He drew Peter closer in order to reveal to him how much He loved him. Peter's love for Jesus may have failed, but Jesus' love for Peter remained as strong as ever.

> *"Who shall bring a charge against God's elect? It is God who justifies. Who is he who condemns? It is Christ who died, and furthermore is also risen, who is even at the right hand of God, who also makes intercession for us. Who shall separate us from the love of Christ? Shall tribulation, or distress, or persecution, or famine, or nakedness, or peril, or sword?"*
> (Romans 8:33-35)

> *"Yet in all these things we are more than conquerors through Him who loved us."*
> (Romans 8:37)

What happened to Peter afterwards? This weak, undependable man became a pillar in the church, a powerful Apostle of Jesus Christ, a writer of two of the books in the Bible, and a martyr for Christ. He started off a failure and ended up more than a conqueror. What a testimony to the power of Jesus' love!

Are you struggling with being faithful today? Consider the outcome of Jesus' dealings with Peter and be encouraged. Know that what the Lord did in Peter's life, He will do for you. When we are faithless, He remains faithful!

> *"Now may the God of peace Himself sanctify you completely; and may your whole spirit, soul, and body be preserved blameless at the coming of our Lord Jesus Christ. He who calls you is faithful, who also will do it."*
> (1 Thessalonians 5:23-24)

Affirm Today:

"I trust You Jesus. I am rejoicing in Your faithfulness and eagerly anticipate that You will accomplish every good thing in my life. I am certain of Your love, and know that I am more than a conqueror because of Your grace."

Additional Scriptures:

Mark 16:7; Romans 8:33; John 16:33; 1 John 5:4; 1 Thessalonians 5:23-24

Day 67

What to Do When You Keep Coming Up Short

D o you ever feel that you do not measure up? That something you desperately desire is beyond your reach? That your best efforts will fall short of the goal? If so, then Luke's account of the meeting that took place between Jesus and a man named Zacchaeus will help you.

A week before His death, Jesus was passing through the city of Jericho. A huge crowd thronged Him. Zacchaeus, the Chief Tax Collector, a very rich man, was one of those eager to see Jesus that day. But there was a problem.

"And he sought to see who Jesus was, but could not because of the crowd, for he was of short stature" (Luke 19:3).

Zacchaeus was too short and the crowd too large. He tried hard to see who Jesus was, a very worthwhile goal, "but he could not." He tried tip-toeing. It did not work. He tried jumping as high as he could. That did not work either. Each time, in spite of the intensity of his desire and the sincerity of his efforts, he came up short. How frustrating!

That would have been enough to send most men home, to cause them to stop trying; to simply give up on their

God-given dream, mission, or assignment. And Zacchaeus could have done the same, but he didn't.

> *"So he ran ahead and climbed up into a syc-amore tree to see Him, for He was going to pass that way."* (Luke 19:4)

Observe what Zacchaeus did in verse 4. He turned the "but" in verse 3 into a "so" in verse 4. And thereby teaches all of us who often come up short a very valuable lesson. Whenever in life you encounter a "but," don't give up. Turn it into a "so."

Child of God, this is one of the most important lessons you will ever learn. Whether it's in your family, your career, or your relationship with God, your dreams will always be challenged by obstacles. "Buts" are inevitable. If you want to reach your goals, achieve your dreams and fulfill your divine purpose in life, you will need to master the art of turning a "but" into a "so."

Now, watch the outcome of Zacchaeus' actions and be encouraged.

> *"And when Jesus came to the place, He looked up and saw him, and said to him, 'Zacchaeus, make haste and come down, for today I must stay at your house.' So he made haste and came down, and received Him joyfully."* (Luke 19:4-6)

Wow, he not only got to see Jesus, he got to spend an entire evening with Jesus by himself at his house! He exceeded his initial goal far beyond his remotest imagination. By turning the "but" into a "so," he transformed a weakness into a strength, an obstacle into an opportunity, and defeat into victory.

Go and do likewise!

Affirm Today:

"I see every obstacle as an opportunity for transformation and victory. My potential is unlimited and my success is sure."

Additional Scriptures:

Luke 19:3-6; Luke 19:9-10; 2 Corinthians 12:9; Hebrews 5:10; Philippians, 4:13

Day 68

Are You Tired?

Life can be draining. Going from where you are to where you need to be is exhausting. Sometimes getting out of bed is the last thing you want to do. I know; I've been there.

But, be encouraged! Listen to these words recorded by the Apostle John.

> *"So He came to a city of Samaria which is called Sychar, near the plot of ground that Jacob gave to his son Joseph. Now Jacob's well was there. Jesus therefore, being wearied from His journey, sat thus by the well. It was about the sixth hour."* (John 4:5-6)

The Message Bible says,
Jesus being *"worn out by the trip, sat down at the well."*

I love to read the miraculous accounts of Jesus walking on the sea, stilling the storm, healing the sick, casting out devils, and multiplying bread and fishes to feed the multitude. Those stories boost my faith and assure me that He is well able to take care of my needs. But to be honest, there are times when I am more blessed by a passage such as this one that shows Jesus' humanity, that reveals His weaknesses and limitations as a human being. I am blessed because I can relate. I have not walked on the water yet, but I know first-hand what it means to be tired and not feel like doing anything but sitting down.

It's good to know feeling this way is not a sin. And, that being human is okay with God. It's good to know Jesus fully understands. He knows tiredness firsthand. It's good to know it does not disqualify me from being a blessing.

> *"For we do not have a high priest who is unable to empathize with our weaknesses, but we have one who has been tempted in every way, just as we are – yet he did not sin."*
> (Hebrews 4:15, NIV)

The good news is because Jesus understands how draining our journey from "Judea to Samaria" can be, He is willing to renew our strength when we are weary. And for this reason, you may turn to Him when you are tired and ask Him for strength. He will help you.

> *"Have you not known? Have you not heard? The everlasting God, the LORD, The Creator of the ends of the earth, Neither faints nor is weary. His understanding is unsearchable. He gives power to the weak, And to those who have no might He increases strength. Even the youths shall faint and be weary, and the young men shall utterly fall; but those who wait on the LORD Shall renew their strength. They shall mount up with wings like eagles; they shall run and not be weary; they shall walk and not faint."* (Isaiah 40:28-31)

Child of God, are you tired? Ask Jesus to refresh you. Then, "sit down at the well" and rest in Him. He will renew your strength. His words are spirit and life.

Affirm Today:

"Lord, I am learning how to wait on You. I am trusting You to renew my strength and I thankfully accept the peace and renewal that only comes from You."

Additional Scriptures:

Hebrews 4:15; Isaiah 40:28-31; Exodus 15:2; Joshua 14:11; John 4:5-6

Day 69

You Don't Have to Be Lukewarm

Do you like lukewarm tea? Lukewarm coffee? I don't. Give me my coffee hot or cold, but lukewarm, and I will spew it out of my mouth. Apparently, the way I feel about lukewarm coffee is the way Jesus feels about lukewarm Christianity.

> *"And to the angel of the church of the Laodiceans write, 'These things says the Amen, the Faithful and True Witness, the Beginning of the creation of God: "I know your works, that you are neither cold nor hot. I could wish you were cold or hot. So then, because you are lukewarm, and neither cold nor hot, I will vomit you out of My mouth."*
> (Revelation 3:14-16)

In choosing to compare the Laodicean Church with lukewarm water, Jesus probably had in mind the cold and hot water springs located in two nearby cities that were therapeutic and sources of healing and refreshing for their citizens. In contrast, lukewarm water provided no such benefit. Unlike these cold and hot springs, the Laodicean Christians were of no benefit to the people of Laodicea. They may have been saved, though this is questionable, but definitely powerless, like salt without its flavor.

Jesus does not like lukewarmness. We are here to make a difference. Sinners need to be saved, sick people need to be healed, oppressed people need to be delivered, families need to be strengthened–and we are the vessels through whom He wants to work to meet these needs! Lukewarmness makes His power of no effect in us.

If you are lukewarm, what is the cure? A rebuke from the Lord, some heartfelt repentance from you, and an intimate relationship with Jesus!

> *"As many as I love, I rebuke and chasten. Therefore be zealous and repent. Behold, I stand at the door and knock. If anyone hears My voice and opens the door, I will come in to him and dine with him, and he with Me."*
> (Revelation 3:19-20)

The number one reason a believer becomes lukewarm is that he or she loses sight of the ever-present Savior and neglects to commune with Him. Without the consciousness of His presence and personal intimacy, we lose our "fire." Faith, hope, and love wane in our lives and our ability to bear His fruit and make a difference in this world follows suit.

Child of God, never lose sight of this gracious reality – Jesus is present with you always. He knocks throughout the day, trying to get your attention. Then, He stands, patiently waiting for your response, hoping you will open the door to Him.

You see, He wants to "dine" with you daily. He yearns to enter into deep communion with you, give you His undivided attention, talk with you about your concerns and share

His thoughts with you. But He must wait; wait until you are ready; ready to give Him your undivided attention.

You may be familiar with the painting of Jesus standing outside on a porch, knocking on a door that has only one handle. A critic said to the artist, "You made a mistake." "No," he said, "this door opens only from the inside."

You don't have to be lukewarm. The intimacy He offers is possible, but only if you want it. Do you? Then open the door.

Affirm Today:

"Lord the fire of our relationship is being rekindled. My adoration for You grows daily as we fellowship together. Your presence is life to me."

Additional Scriptures:

Revelation 3:19-20; Exodus 36:2; Deuteronomy 4:29; Psalm 27:8; Revelation 3:14-16

Day 70

You Are Not Still In Your Sins

Guilty or not guilty? Detectives look for clues. Lawyers seek to convince. Juries ask for proof. The stronger the evidence, the more reliable the facts, the more certain the verdict. We make bold claims concerning the sacrifice of Jesus. Do we have solid Biblical evidence to support our claim that because we believe in the blood of Jesus we are totally and absolutely not guilty before God of sin? Yes!

> *"And if Christ is not risen, your faith is futile;
> you are still in your sins!"* (1 Corinthians 15:17)

Let's look at this verse. Let's analyze it. Then, make some logical deductions.

First, what does it mean to be "still" in your sins? It does not mean you are still capable of sinning and still do. If that were the case, there would be no one who is not "still" in his or her sins. Rather, this expression means to be still under the sentence of judgment because of your sins. It means that you are still being charged for your sins and are still subject to divine punishment for breaking God's laws.

211

Now, let's engage in a bit of logic. If A = B, then B = A. It used to be so when I was in junior high. Unless things have changed, it still is. Logic is still logic.

According to this verse, if Christ be not risen, even though we have faith, we are still in our sins, i.e. subject to divine judgement because of our sins. Since this statement is true, then logically, the opposite idea has to be equally true. So let's consider the opposite statement.

If we are still in our sins, even though we have faith, then Christ is not risen. This is worth re-phrasing. If, as some say, we who have faith in Christ are still in our sins, then we must conclude that Christ is not risen as we claim.

The two ideas, Christ being risen and believers still being in their sins are, logically speaking, mutually exclusive. It's either one or the other. It is biblically illogical and spiritually impossible for both statements to be true. Either Christ is risen, or we are in our sins. You must accept one or the other.

Is Christ risen? He is. The grave is empty.

Then, can you, who believe in Him, still be "in your sins?" Absolutely not!

Listen to Paul reiterate this truth elsewhere.

> *"Now it was not written for his sake alone*
> *that it was imputed to him, but also for us.*
> *It shall be imputed to us who believe in Him*
> *who raised up Jesus our Lord from the dead,*
> *who was delivered up because of our offenses,*
> *and was raised because of our justification."*
> (Romans 4:23-25)

According to verse 25, Jesus was raised because of our justification. That is, the resurrection of Jesus was due to and on account of us being justified. It was predicated upon Jesus successfully making us holy, righteous and blameless before God. Had He failed to take out of the way just one of our sins,

He would have failed to make us blameless in the eyes of the Law. God, then, would not have raised Him up from death. It would have been spiritually illegal for Him to do so.

We, therefore, conclude thus: all our sin debts are forever settled and all charges dismissed. We are totally and completely forgiven once for all time. The Lamb of God has succeeded in taking all our sins out of the way. And what is our proof? The resurrection of Jesus!

Child of God, are you willing to say that Jesus is not risen? Then neither should you be willing to say that you, who believe in Him, are still in your sins, subject to God's wrath for your sins. To say this, for all practical purposes, is to deny the resurrection of Jesus Christ!

Thank God, Christ is risen! Thank God, I am no longer in my sins! Thank God, I now have indwelling power, because I am not in my sins, to live like a king and a priest unto my Father! Thank God for His grace!

Affirm Today:

"I am sinless, forgiven, and free. I am alive in Jesus Christ, a king and a priest. Daily my new life is being revealed."

Additional Scriptures:

Romans 4:23-25; John 8:36; Romans 8:2; Galatians 5:1; 1 Corinthians 15:17

Day 71

Are You Facing Trouble?

Trouble comes in different sizes. Some are small enough for you to ignore. Others are meager enough for you to manage alone. But what do you do when you are surrounded by an army of trouble? That was the question the servant of Elisha wanted an answer to the morning an army of trouble came looking for them.

He got up early that morning as was his custom. He had had a good night's rest. The sun was up and the day looked bright. So there was no reason to suspect that this would be anything but a good day. But he was in for a surprise, and not a very pretty one! When he stepped outside, he noticed something that scared him so much, he may have wet himself. An entire army of Syrian soldiers, equipped with horses and chariots, had surrounded him and Elisha. An army of trouble had come looking for them and they were found!

Do you know what it's like for an army of trouble to come looking for you? What it feels like to be surrounded by trouble? You know an army of trouble has located you when trouble shows up everywhere, in your marriage, in your checkbook, in your children, in you ministry, in your workplace. And all of these things are happening at the same time!

Your spouse is not acting right, and while you are trying to deal with that, you get a call from the school that your son hasn't been showing up for classes, and while you are trying to deal with that the car breaks down. Now you've got to come up with money you don't have to fix it. It's just one thing after another. On top of all this, the doctor just diagnosed you with a serious illness.

"Alas, my master, what shall we do?" the servant exclaimed," (2 Kings 6:15). He was very worried and afraid. You would be too, unless you knew what Elisha knew.

Notice how different Elisha's response was.

> *"So he answered, 'Do not fear, for those who are with us are more than those who are with them.' And Elisha prayed, and said, 'Lord, I pray, open his eyes that he may see.' Then the Lord opened the eyes of the young man, and he saw. And behold, the mountain was full of horses and chariots of fire all around Elisha."*
> (2 Kings 6:16-17)

Here is the Apostle John's version of the same spiritual reality.

> *"You are of God, little children, and have overcome them, because He who is in you is greater than he who is in the world."*
> (1 John 4:4)

Child of God, when trouble comes, what will you be saying? "Oh no, oh no, no, no, what shall I do?" Or will you be able to say calmly and confidently, "I see trouble everywhere, but I know there are more with me than there are with them. I know greater is He who is in me than everything that is against me."

Are you facing trouble today? Be encouraged. Even if you are surrounded by an entire army of it, you do not need to worry or be afraid. Why? There will always be more for you than those against you. And the One who dwells in you will always be greater than that which is in the world.

The truth is, your troubles are in trouble!

Affirm Today:

"I release fear, worry, and instead welcome victorious living. I am an overcomer because greater is He that is in me than he who is in the world. Thank you Jesus!"

Additional Scriptures:

1 John 4:4; Psalm 121:1-2; John 10:10; Psalm 18:10; 2 Kings 6:16-17

Day 72

Who Are You?

So who are you? If you have received Jesus as Savior, you are a "son of God."

> *"But as many as did receive him to them he gave authority to become sons of God – to those believing in his name, who – not of blood nor of a will of flesh, nor of a will of man but – of God were begotten."* (John 1:12-13, YLT)

> *"For it was fitting for Him, for whom are all things, and through whom are all things, in bringing many sons to glory, to perfect the author of their salvation through sufferings. For both He who sanctifies and those who are sanctified are all from one Father; for which reason He is not ashamed to call them brethren."* (Hebrews 2:10-11, NASB)

Wow, Jesus is no longer the only begotten Son of God! We are the sons of God also. Even as Jesus is, we "of God were begotten". Now, every believer, like Jesus, can say with absolute integrity and truthfulness, "I am born of God and I have 'son of God' life inside of me. God is my Father. I have His nature and His ability within."

Now, let this truth sink in. When you received Jesus as your Savior, you became one of God's "begotten sons." You received brand new spiritual genes. Your spirit was made new and divine. You are not God, but you are God-like. You now carry "son of God" life inside of you.

Child of God, renew your mind to see yourself as you are in Christ. Start acknowledging you are "a begotten son of God". Understand the life you carry inside of you is God's and it is invincible. Then face every test, every temptation, declaring your confidence in and being grateful for the sufficiency and the invincibility of the divine life working in you. This is what makes you more than a conqueror. This is God's gift to you, courtesy of Jesus!

Affirm Today:

"I believe and accept that I am a son of God and I feel wonderful. God is my Father. I have His incredible nature and His ability. My life reflects His glory. I am grateful for the sufficiency and invincibility of His divine life working in me. In every situation I am more than a conqueror."

Additional Scriptures:

Hebrews 2:10-11; Romans 8:14; Romans 9:26; 2 Corinthians 6:18; John 1:12-13

Day 73

Free to Choose

You know the story. God made man in His own image. Then said to him, *"Adam, of all the trees in the Garden you may eat, except of the tree of the knowledge of good and evil. The day you eat of it you will surely die"* (Genesis 2:16-17). This was no threat. Just a warning. An act of love. Similar to when a wise and loving mother says to her grown son, "Stay away from that girl. She's no good."

He did not listen. He ate anyway. He chose separation over union. Independence over dependence. And just as God warned, he died. Spiritually. Then physically.

Choices have consequences. Disease, death, darkness. Sin, suffering, Satan. These are the results of Adam's choice. And ours. Not God's!

But couldn't God have made Adam do right? Yes. Should God have done so? No. Why? Simple. A human being with choice, even if he does wrong, is superior to a robot with no choice, even if he does right.

God chose to make man in His own image. He did not make a robot. He was too loving to do so. God is free. Man is free.

Man chose wrongly. Man fell profoundly. God chose again.

"For God so loved the world that He gave His only begotten Son, that whoever believes in Him should not perish but have everlasting life. For God did not send His Son into the world to condemn the world, but that the world through Him might be saved."
(John 3:16-17)

He sent His Son to save the world. To restore what was lost. To regenerate what had died. To reclaim what was forfeited. To do so on behalf of man, who will always be, the apple of His eye, the subject of His love, the object of His choosing.

Child of God, the Father loves you, and for that reason, He continually chooses to be good to you. That is amazing. But just like He did not force Adam, He will not force you to receive His love. Yet, He yearns for you to choose it for yourself, daily. He wants to pour it out upon you in great abundance.

You are not a robot. You are free to receive God's love in Christ. Please do.

Affirm Today:

"Jesus I choose You. I relinquish my own independence and choose total dependence on You. I let go of everything else and renew my mind by Your word. I am restored, the apple of God's eye, chosen and divinely loved. This is my destiny."

Additional Scriptures:

Luke 2:11; John 4:42; 1 Timothy 4:10; John 3:16-17; Philippians 3:30

Day 74

The Problem of Evil

Have you ever heard someone blame God for evil? Just the other day I heard a Christian lady, distressed about the senseless murder of her friend by a suicidal man high on drugs, say, "I don't know why God took him like that. He was such a good person." My heart grieved. God took him?

Friend, God is good all the time. He does not commit murder. He does not destroy human life. God did not kill her friend. A crazy man, influenced by drugs and devils, did.

Now, if her friend was trusting in Jesus as his Savior, then he was a child of God. And the good news is that God's born-again children never die. They have eternal life. Instead of murdering him, God was there to welcome him and usher him into Paradise. God is good.

James writes:

> *"Do not err, my beloved brethren. Every good gift and every perfect gift is from above, and cometh down from the Father of lights, with whom is no variableness, neither shadow of turning."* (James 1:16-17)

The evil that is in this world is the result of sin and disobedience to God. And unfortunately, innocent people do suffer sometimes because of their lack of knowledge, the harmful choices of others, and the evil influences Satan has upon society. This is sad, but this is the consequence of living in a world where men, who are free to obey or not to obey God, often choose the path of disobedience.

This was what happened in the case of Joseph. He was betrayed by his own brothers, sold as a slave and imprisoned falsely for a crime he did not commit. But in all that Joseph went through, he did not blame God. He knew that God was not the source of evil. He continued to submit to and place his trust in the goodness of God. And though times were tough and his suffering lasted a long time, God was with him through it all. In the end, God turned it around and richly rewarded Joseph's faith.

So what should we do when we are confronted with evil and suffering? Let's not err and blame God. Instead, let's give thanks to Him for being the good God He is. Let's acknowledge that every good and perfect gift comes from our loving Heavenly Father. Then let's choose to submit to Him because He is good and resist the devil because he is evil. And let's be confident that ultimately good will triumph over evil!

Affirm Today:

"Lord I submit to and place my confidence in Your unchanging goodness. I steadfastly resist the devil because he is evil and I am confident that ultimately good will triumph over evil."

Additional Scriptures:

Numbers 23:19; Psalm 27:13; Psalm 33:5; Exodus 33:19; James 1:16-17

Day 75

All You Need Is Grace

Do you know what God's answer to all your weaknesses, shortcomings, and inadequacies is? It is His grace!

Listen to what the Apostle said in 1 Corinthians 15:10: *"I am what I am by the grace of God."* Now, think about this. This was the Apostle's testimony: "I am not what I am today because of my extensive experience, first-class education, wonderful upbringing, great national heritage. I am what I am by the grace of God!"

Paul had one explanation for his success – God's grace. Grace made him the man he had become and grace empowered him to do what he had done. And that same grace will make you! What you could never do or be because of your shortcomings, you can be and do by the grace of God.

Romans 6:14 reads, *"For sin shall not be master over you, for you are not under law, but under grace."*

Men succeed under grace, who fail under law. Why? Because the man who is under law is trying to work for God, but the man who is under grace has God working for him! No wonder he succeeds. You see, grace is God's ability at work – at work for us, in us and through us, even though we do not deserve it.

My spiritual son, Reverend Patrick Wleh, writes:

"Grace is not in search of good and clean men whom it can approve. On the contrary, grace does not approve goodness; only justice does. But rather grace is in search of the condemned, guilty, speechless and helpless, whom it can save, sanctify, and glorify...Where grace is at work, every other law is disabled!"

Grace is at work when we are trusting in Jesus and not in ourselves.

> *"And of His fullness have all we received and grace for grace. For the law was given through Moses, but grace and truth came through Jesus Christ."* (John 1:16-17)

Are you conscious of how weak and needy you are? Are you facing impossible circumstances? The grace of God is your answer. And His grace is available without measure through Jesus Christ, God's Son, our Savior.

Affirm Today:

"Because of grace I am free to live boldly, bravely, holy and fully accepted by God. Jesus I see Your glorious grace working in my life. Thank You!"

Additional Scriptures:

Romans 6:14; John 1:16-17; Romans 5:15; Romans 5:2; 1 Corinthians 15:10

Day 76

Parenting God's Way

What is the solution to not provoking our children? It is to "bring them up in the nurture and admonition of the Lord." *"And you, fathers, do not provoke your children to wrath, but bring them up in the training and admonition of the Lord"* (Ephesians 6:4). Our Heavenly Father is a lover and an encourager. So, if our children are becoming resentful and discouraged as the result of our words and actions, we are not bringing them up His way. But if parents do it God's way, their children will feel very loved and immensely encouraged.

The Scriptures teach the job of parents is to "nourish" their children. This means parents are expected to provide the things their children need to grow and be healthy. And since children are spiritual and emotional beings, their needs are not only physical. As important as their physical needs are, it is inadequate to focus only on making sure they have food to eat, clothes to wear, and a bed to sleep in.

While children need to feel physically safe, every child also needs to feel emotionally secure and spiritually significant, as well. Now, God intends the relationship parents have with their children to be the primary conduit by which these other needs get met. Children with parents who neglect their need for emotional security and spiritual significance will require a miracle of grace to grow normally and function healthily.

Just like a plant needs a certain type of soil in which to flourish, children grow best when their parents give them love, limits, and latitude. All children should get up each day feeling loved unconditionally, knowing that even when Mom and Dad are displeased with their behavior, their commitment to them is unwavering. All children should get up every day, knowing their parents will protect them and teach them self-control by establishing and lovingly enforcing appropriate limits for their good. And all children should get up every day, knowing their parents will give them enough latitude to be themselves, unique and different, as they discover and fulfill their special purpose in God's wonderful plan for their family and the world. Giving children reasonable latitude, based on their maturity and disposition, equips them to self-direct and to govern themselves later in life, when their parents won't be around.

Admittedly, parenting is difficult. But God's grace is sufficient. Parents can place their faith in Him and daily allow His love, His strength, and His wisdom to work in them. And when they miss it, as they may do from time to time, know His super-abundant grace will cause all things to work together for the good of those who love Him.

I pray for all parents, and all children, that they may be filled with the knowledge of God's will, and that they may know experientially the love of God that passes knowledge so that they may be filled with the fullness of God.

Affirm Today:

"I nourish my children in Godly ways. I am equipped to help them experience God's love as I teach, guide and nurture them. I am strong and establish right limits to guide them.

226

They are sure of my love and best intentions for their good, no matter what."

Additional Scriptures:

Psalm 34:11; Genesis 27:8; Deuteronomy 5:16; Ephesians 6:4; Psalm 127:3-5

Day 77

Before You Say "I Do"

W hat type of marriage do you want? *"Therefore a man shall leave his father and mother and be joined to his wife, and they shall become one flesh"* (Genesis 2:24). One lady said that she got married looking for the ideal, but ended up with an ordeal and now she wants a new deal. The good news is, if you do marriage God's way, you'll be blessed with the ideal, and you won't be asking for a new deal.

Tony Evans writes, "For many people, marriage is like a three-ring circus. First, there is the engagement ring. Next comes the wedding ring. Then, there is suffering." That's not what God has planned for you. Instead of suffering, he wants your marriage to be an offering to Him, and a blessing to you and others.

Now, if you want a marriage that will honor God, one built on a foundation strong enough to weather the storms, one that like wine will get better with time, one that pursues holiness instead of happiness and ends up with both, one that your children and grandchildren will be proud of and want to emulate, the best time to start working on it is before you say, "I do". You may have heard the statement "Everybody will end up somewhere. Only a few get there on purpose." How true! You are going to end up somewhere, but if you leave that to chance, you will most likely end up where you do not want to be.

Applying this truth to marriage means you need to be wise and purposeful in making decisions regarding your relationships now, and not leave this to chance. Start paying attention to yourself and to your decisions before marriage, because paying attention will determine your direction and your ultimate destination. You should be intentional in choosing your friends, but extraordinarily so in choosing your spouse.

Do not marry someone just because he or she is good looking, or popular, or you have "fallen in love." Emotional decisions are seldom good decisions. Be led by wisdom and let your emotions follow. Otherwise, you are likely to end up with buyer's remorse.

Once, I needed to be in Houston. It would have been crazy for me to have gone to the airport, and boarded the first plane because it was the nearest and easiest one to get on, or because it was the prettiest of all the planes – the logo, paint job, and external design were just superb. No, when I am planning to fly, I am not concerned about the external paint job of the plane, and I don't care what colors it is painted with or the design of its logo. What I am concerned about is the internal structure and mechanical engineering of the plane, the skill of the pilot, the time it departs and arrives, and the airport it is flying to. It would be crazy to decide to board a plane based on the paint job.

It is also crazy for you to be willing to get on board the "love plane" and "take off" with someone on a journey in marriage, just because he or she has a good "paint job", and you like the external design. Wisdom would dictate you be far more concerned about their internal structure and engineering to determine whether or not they have the character and relationship skills, not only to "take off" with you, but to be able to fly in good weather and through turbulence, and that you know in advance at what "airport" they intend to land. It is crazy to be willing to embark upon a life-altering journey with another person and not be certain about the direction he or she wants to take you in, or the final destination he or she has in mind, but to hope that somehow you will arrive where you need to be, just because you "love" or are "attracted" to that person.

I have met and counseled too many hurting people who decided to marry on the basis of a "paint job" and "external design" and now are utterly miserable. Too many make up their minds without seriously taking into account the wisdom and counsel of the Lord in choosing a mate, and when they do "consult" the Lord, it is only to get His approval for what they have already decided.

Let me give you some personal advice to help you. God is a lot wiser than you. He's been around much longer than you have, loves you more than you love yourself. The best thing you can do for yourself is to pay attention to what He says and the guidance He has already given in His Word about many issues regarding you, including the ones relating to marriage. And start paying attention now, before you say "I do."

Affirm Today:

"Thank You Father. I am depending on You to help me joyfully choose the right mate who will glorify You and love me like Christ loved the Church. I am certain of Your good provision for this area of my life and anticipate the intimate, sanctioned relationship that is coming."

Additional Scriptures:

Genesis 2:24; Luke 20:34; Hebrews 13:4; 1 Corinthians 7:36; 1 Timothy 5:14

Day 78

Going From Glory to Glory

A re you concerned about the changes taking place around you? Are you afraid of where your life is headed? Well, if you belong to Christ, don't be. His Word assures us that God changes us "from glory to glory."

> *"But we all, with unveiled face, beholding as*
> *in a mirror the glory of the Lord, are being*
> *transformed into the same image from glory*
> *to glory, just as by the Spirit of the Lord."*
> (2 Corinthians 3:18)

We see here that the Holy Spirit is in charge of effecting changes in the lives of the children of God, and we are told, He changes us from "glory to glory." Not from "glory to garbage." That means, we can count on Him to move us forward, not backwards. He will always change us for the better.

And this is true, even when it does not appear to be the case. He was moving Joseph forward, even when he was sold as a slave by his brothers, lied upon by Potiphar's wife, and falsely imprisoned for a crime he did not commit. That was his route to the palace.

He was moving Moses from glory to glory, even when he was fleeing from Egypt to live in the desert for forty years. He was actually on the way to becoming the leader and deliverer of Israel. That was his route to greatness.

And He was moving Jesus forward, even when he was being betrayed by Judas, deserted by His disciples and cruci- fied by His enemies. He was on His way to the right hand of the Father to be Lord and to become the Source of Salvation for the world.

Child of God, do not be afraid of changes, or worry about where your life is headed. Just keep beholding the beauty of Jesus daily, as your righteousness, as your Savior. Then you can rest in His promise that the Holy Spirit will change you from glory to glory. And He will!

Remember, you are not moving backwards, no matter what it looks like. He is moving you forward.

Affirm Today:

"I move forward in every area of my life and welcome the changes God brings. I receive fresh revelation as I trust and obey."

Additional Scriptures:

1 Corinthians 3:18; Genesis 41:39-43; Hebrews 11:24-27; Hebrews 12:2; Jeremiah 12:11

Day 79

The Resurrection of Jesus: Fraud, Fiction, or Fact

Our sin nature is eradicated, our sins are evaporated, and our guilt is eliminated. That is, if Jesus arose. We believe He did. Skeptics say He did not. If Jesus Christ did not rise, He is the greatest fraud to have ever lived, the Gospel is pure fiction, and the future of humankind is hopeless. We are still in our sins. But if He did arise, we are blessed, blessed, and blessed again!

Since there is monumental evidence for the resurrection, the burden is on those who deny the resurrection of Jesus Christ to prove it did not occur. What evidence do they have that it did not happen? The truth is they reject the resurrection, not because they have objectively examined the evidence as a judge would do in a court of law, but because they have concluded, without proof, that miracles do not happen. This is not science; this is a philosophical bias.

Miracles do happen. Though they will not admit it, even evolutionary science is based on a miracle. It is an axiom of science that anything that has a beginning must have a cause outside of itself. Since the universe had a beginning, it could not have caused or created itself. That would be a scientific absurdity. The universe, therefore, could not have come into existence without the outside intervention of a force strong enough to begin it and which of necessity had to be in existence already. Thus, evolutionary science is based on a miracle.

Once we accept the possibility of miracles, the evidence for the resurrection is significant, far more than would be required in a court of law to reach a verdict beyond any reasonable doubt. Consider the following:

1. The credibility of Christ
Jesus claimed publicly He would be killed and on the third day arise. Who in his right mind would make such an "impossible" claim and expect people to take him seriously, unless He was very confident He could fulfill that promise? No wonder no other religious leader dared to make such a promise. Had He failed to deliver, Jesus would have lost all credibility and not only He, but Christianity itself would have died with Him. But Christianity did not die, and that's because Jesus arose.

2. The courage of the disciples
Shortly after His arrest, they were filled with fear. They denied Him and fled for their lives. They lacked both the courage and the conviction required to remain loyal when their very lives were on the line. But just a short while later, they stood boldly in the temple and on the streets proclaiming Jesus as Lord, prepared to pay for this message with their own blood. What can account for this profound psychological transformation and behavioral change in all eleven of these men in only a few days? Only one thing, the resurrection! They testify that they became convinced when He appeared to them personally on several occasions after He arose.

3. The confirmation of eyewitnesses

The strength of the eyewitness testimonies alone should be enough to prove Jesus arose. If a lawyer in our judicial system can produce just two or three credible eyewitnesses to testify they saw and heard the same thing that would be considered more than enough evidence to prove his case beyond a reasonable doubt. In the case of the resurrection, we have at least 514 persons testifying that they saw Him, some of them heard Him, touched Him, and even had breakfast and dinner with Him. What motive did they have to fabricate a story like this one? In their Jewish cultural setting, these men and women had nothing to gain by lying, and much to lose by telling the truth. Not one or two, but 514 persons willing to testify and die for a lie they made up? That is just not logical!

4. The condition of the tomb

The tomb of Jesus is empty. Who moved the body? His enemies would not. His friends could not. His disciples did not. We are left with only one other possibility.

Saints, Jesus arose. Sinners, Jesus arose. Saints and sinners, He arose for you. He arose because He is the Son of God. He arose that you might arise also.

Believe on Him now and you shall arise also!

Affirm Today:

"Jesus, I believe You are the miracle that happened. I know Your life is true and You did not lie. And I am convinced and certain that You arose from the dead. Because You live, I live also. You are my Savior. You are my Lord. Thank You, I am grateful for Your life and what You accomplished for me on the cross."

Additional Scriptures:

Revelation 1:18; 1 Corinthians 15:16; Acts 1:9-11; John 20:11-17; Matthew 28:2-7

Day 80

Don't Let Them Fool You

"Truth is relative. All religions are the same. All that matters is that you do what makes you happy and you treat other people right. As long as you are sincere, God understands." You've probably heard people express these sentiments. It's becoming more and more popular to talk and think this way. But don't be fooled!

If you drink a glass of poison because you sincerely believe it's a glass of milk, your sincerity won't save you. You may still die. When it comes to your physical life, what you drink matters!

And so it is with your soul. What you believe matters! Dead religion, atheism, and humanism are deadly poisons. Swallow them, they kill, no matter how sincere you are.

Jesus said, *"I am the Way, the Truth, and the Life. No man comes to the Father except through Me"* (John 14:6). Believe this and you will live with God, forever!

"Why," you ask, "should I accept His Word?" Consider this. The Romans killed Him. He said they would. And He said on Day Three He would rise again. He did. An empty tomb is there to prove it. He has a track record of always telling the truth and of doing things only God could do.

Oh, there's another reason you should believe in Him! He loves you and is going to return to receive you so that where He is, you may be also.

Don't let them fool you. What you believe matters! Receive Jesus as your Lord and Savior today, and you shall be saved.

Affirm Today:

"I abandon the wisdom of the world and accept the wisdom of God. Jesus is the Way, the Truth, and the Life. I believe and I know what matters. Jesus matters and where He is I am."

Additional Scriptures:

John 14:6; 2 Timothy 3:16; Psalm 53:1-3; John 2:23; Matthew 28:7

Day 81

Eat the Meal that Heals

She was diagnosed with herpes. Doctors told her there was no cure. She asked Jesus to heal her. And she started to take communion, daily, for her healing. Each day, she ate the bread and drank the grape juice, confessing, "By His stripes we are healed." She did so for months. Then she returned to the doctor. New tests were ordered. No trace of herpes. Totally healed. The doctors were wrong. There was a cure. This meal heals!

The Lord's Supper, or covenant meal, is more than a memorial. The bread and wine are more than mere symbols. The Holy Spirit uses them to convey divine life and power to our bodies. They are what theologians refer to as "means of grace."

Moses' rod was a means of grace. With it, God parted the Red Sea. Peter's shadow and Paul's clothing were means of grace as well. With them, God healed the sick, drove out demons, and worked miracles.

In 1 Corinthians 11, Paul directs our attention to the power of this meal to heal. Believers were sick and some had died prematurely because they failed to "discern the Lord's body." Not recognizing the power of the Lord to heal that is present in the covenant meal, they expected nothing and received nothing. What a loss.

In Genesis 2, Adam was told he would die if he ate of the tree of the knowledge of good and evil. But in John 6, the disciples are told they would live if they ate of the Bread of Life. Both death and life are the result of eating.

> *"This is the bread which comes down from heaven, that one may eat of it and not die. I am the living bread which came down from heaven. If anyone eats of this bread, he will live forever; and the bread that I shall give is My flesh, which I shall give for the life of the world."* (John 6:50-51)

Adam ate from the wrong tree and died. If we eat from the right tree, we will live.

> *"As the living Father sent Me, and I live because of the Father, so he who feeds on Me will live because of Me. This is the bread which came down from heaven—not as your fathers ate the manna, and are dead. He who eats this bread will live forever."* (John 6:57-58)

Jesus is the Bread of Life. Partake of Him wholeheartedly, partake daily, partake confidently and patiently. And as you do so, confess your faith that His body and blood cleanses you from all your sins and heals you from all you diseases.

Beloved, this is the meal that heals. Eat and be made whole!

Affirm Today:

"Jesus, Your body and blood cleanses me from all sin and every disease. I accept communion in faith and receive Your divine healing power. Thank You!"

Additional Scriptures:

John 6:50-51; John 6:57-58; Genesis 2:17; 1 Corinthians 11:24; John 6:51; John 6:58

Day 82

Do This And Live

The stench of death filled the air. The snakes were biting. People were dying. And they kept dying until God revealed the cure. "Do this and you will live!"

Do what?

> *"Make a bronze serpent and hang it on a pole. Then if anyone is bitten, let that one look at the bronze serpent and he will live."* (Numbers 21:9)

And they did and they lived!

In the New Testament, Jesus compared himself to this bronze serpent.

> *"No one has ascended to heaven but He who came down from heaven, that is, the Son of Man who is in heaven. And as Moses lifted up the serpent in the wilderness, even so must the Son of Man be lifted up, that whoever believes*

in Him should not perish but have eternal life."
(John 3:13-15)

The bronze serpent on a pole is a type of the Son of God being judged in our place for all our sins and taking upon himself the curses we deserved. It reveals how the power of the serpent to harm us is neutralized by the work Jesus did on the cross.

Today, if you are "bitten" in your soul, mind, or body by the serpents of sin, sickness, or poverty, you do not have to die or be overcome by their poison. God has provided a remedy for the serpent's bite. It's the finished work of Jesus on the cross. That's where the heads of "serpents" are crushed and their poison neutralized.

Child of God, you do not need to be afraid of the serpent's bite any more. Keep meditating daily on how Jesus overcame every curse for you on the cross. Then if you ever feel the sting of the serpent's bite, do not worry. Just remember to look attentively and confidently at the finished work of the cross and ask for a fresh revelation of the victory Jesus has already obtained for you.

Do this and you will live.

Affirm Today:

"I am a joyful recipient of the finished work of Jesus Christ on the cross. I live fearlessly and walk in victory. Success in life is my inheritance and my eyes are on Jesus, the author and finisher of my faith."

Additional Scriptures:

John 3:13-15; Numbers 21:8-9; John 3:16-17; Act 10:38; Act 17:28

Day 83

Life at Its Best

From the way people talk and many Christians act, you would think Jesus came to found a cemetery and make us as much like dead people as possible. Ask a typical person who a Christian is and don't be surprised if he tells you a Christian is someone who does not smoke, drink, cuss or fornicate. But if that is what makes a person a Christian, then the place to find the best Christians in town is in the local cemetery because you will not find joy there, and you will never catch them cussing, smoking, drinking, or fornicating.

Now, no sincere Christian will practice sin since grace teaches him or her to say no to ungodliness and worldly lusts. But a person is not a Christian just because he or she does not do certain things. And the church is not a cemetery filled with lifeless people!

To the contrary, Jesus came to give life to the dead. Listen to Him speak:

> *"The thief did not come but to steal, kill and destroy, but I have come that they may have life and that more abundantly."* (John 10:10)

It could not be more clear. He came to make dead men live. He came so that men would experience life "more abundantly."

Jesus is using a superlative to help us understand how full a life He came to give us. Abundant life is life that is fuller than full, greater than great, and better than best. It is a life that has both earthly significance and eternal ramifications. It is life that is both challenging and immensely satisfying.

The source of abundant life is Jesus Himself. *"I am the way, the truth, and the life,"* He said. *"No one comes to the Father except through Me"* (John 14:6). And later John writes in 1 John 5:12, *"He who has the Son has life."*

Here we find the true definition of a Christian and he is not merely one who does not practice sin. No, he is much more than that. He is the person who has the Son–that is, the one into whom Jesus has come, and through whom Jesus is living.

And that my friend, Jesus living and working in you, both to will and do His good pleasure, is life at its best. No, it's life that is better than best! It's life abundant.

A bumper sticker I read some time ago captures this truth well. "No Jesus, no life. Know Jesus, know life."

I am glad I accepted His offer of life years ago and started to look to Him daily to live through me. What a difference He has made for me! I know He can do the same for you too.

Affirm Today:

"My life is fuller than full, greater than great, and better than best. I am living the abundant life."

Additional Scriptures:

John 10:10; 1 John 5:12; John 14:6; John 1:16; Ephesians 1:3

Day 84

The Power in Your Mouth

D o you know that with your words you can cause things
to live and things to die? That your success in life is con-
nected to what you say out of your mouth? Your tongue is
the most powerful member of your body. The power of death
and life is actually in your mouth.

Listen to these words from the Bible.

> *"A man's stomach shall be satisfied from the
> fruit of his mouth; from the produce of his
> lips he shall be filled. Death and life are in
> the power of the tongue, and those who love
> it will eat its fruit."* (Proverbs 18:20-21)

One day Jesus cursed a fig tree, saying to it, *"No man will
eat fruit from you again."* And His disciples heard Him. The
next day as they passed by, they exclaimed, *"Master, the fig
tree you cursed is withered from the roots."* Then Jesus said
unto them, *"Truly, I say to you, whosoever shall say to this
mountain, 'Be uprooted and cast into the sea and does not
doubt in his heart but believes the things he says shall come*

to pass, he shall have whatsoever he says'" (Mark 11:14, 20, 22-24).

The book of James compares the tongue to the rudder of a ship, the bit in the horse's mouth, and a small fire started in a forest. With a tiny rudder, a captain controls the direction of a massive ship, and with a tiny bit, the horseman tells the horse where to go and it obeys. And who can deny the destructive power of a little spark of fire set in a forest! The tongue, says James, though tiny, is as powerful and influential in determining the course and destiny of your life as any of these.

That is why Hebrews 10:23 exhorts us to *"hold fast the confession of our hope without wavering, for He who promised is faithful"* (Hebrews 10:23). The word translated "confession" literally means, "to say the same thing." God wants to give us a glorious future and for us to experience every promise He has made and fulfilled in Christ. And we will, if we yield our tongues to Him and allow Him to bring our tongues under His influence.

Child of God, God has a wonderful plan for your life. The Holy Spirit stands ready to confirm every promise of God made to you and fulfilled in Jesus. The course He has set for you to follow leads to life and more life. But He needs your cooperation because whoever controls your tongue gets to control your life and determine the direction it moves in.

So, let the Word of Christ dwell in you richly. Meditate on His message of love and grace continually and let it fill your heart and mouth daily. By so doing, your tongue will become a fountain of life and you will begin to enjoy the abundant life Jesus died to provide for you.

And that's the way it should be!

Affirm Today:

"Lord, teach me how, what, and when to speak. Give me wisdom to speak life and not death. I am ready to change and learn from You."

Additional Scriptures:

Proverbs 18:20-21; Mark 11:22-24; Hebrews 10:23; 2 Samuel 23:2; Philippians 4:8

Day 85

It Does Not Have to Be This Way

His birth was painful. Everyone said his life would be a failure. He was to be a sorrow-maker. His parents believed this too. They named him Jabez. Jabez means pain.

But he proved them wrong. Very wrong. He became the one his family looked up to. They even named a city after him.

> *"And Jabez was more honorable than his brethren: and his mother called his name Jabez, saying, Because I bare him with sorrow. And Jabez called on the God of Israel, saying, "Oh that thou wouldest bless me indeed, and enlarge my coast, and that thine hand might be with me, and that thou wouldest keep me from evil, that it may not grieve me!" And God granted him that which he requested."* (1 Chronicles 4:9-10, KJV)

Jabez overcame adversity. He changed his story. He altered the plot. He became great. How? He prayed to the God of Israel. That's the power of prayer!

Prayer can change your story. You may not always be able to determine how things begin, but by tapping into God's love and grace through prayer, you can influence how your story ends.

I have come to realize that by passionate, believing prayer, I allow God to rewrite the script, to alter the story line, to introduce some new characters, to get involved in the conflicts, to manipulate the details of my story to ensure that the climax is always for my good and for His glory.

God is a master storyteller. The best writers are able to keep the readers in suspense until the very end. There are things they allow the reader to hear and see, but then hidden behind all that is heard and seen is another story that is not revealed until the very end. That's the kind of writer God is. Let Him finish your story for you.

Who said you cannot have a bad beginning and a good ending? Who said it has to be this way? Child of God, pray!

Affirm Today:

"I know in Whom I have believed and You Lord are able to keep me, bless me, and make my life a success."

Additional Scriptures:

1 Chronicles 4:9-10; Jeremiah 29:11-12; Acts 20:32; Ephesians 1:11; Luke 12:32

Day 86

Jesus Will Turn It Around

"**D**o not believe it when your mind tells you it's over. Just because it looks bad today does not mean it will be bad tomorrow. Ruth is a witness.

> *"Then the women said to Naomi, "Blessed be the LORD, who has not left you this day without a close relative; and may his name be famous in Israel! And may he be to you a restorer of life and a nourisher of your old age; for your daughter-in-law, who loves you, who is better to you than seven sons, has borne him." Then Naomi took the child and laid him on her bosom, and became a nurse to him. Also the neighbor women gave him a name, saying, "There is a son born to Naomi." And they called his name Obed. He is the father of Jesse, the father of David." (Ruth 4:14-17)*

Her past was horrendous. Her present dismal. Her future bleak. At least that's how Ruth was feeling about life. Ten years earlier, her mother-in-law, Naomi, had left Israel for

Moab to escape a famine with her husband and two sons. Now, tragically, she was returning home a widow and childless, with nothing to her name. Her husband and both of her sons had died. Ruth, her loyal daughter-in-law, was accompanying her on her journey, a young, childless widow herself.

Both Naomi and Ruth felt their lives were over. They saw no joy in their future. But this was not the end of the story. You see, when God is in the picture, the story is never over until His child wins.

What happened next? Ruth went out to find food, and she just "happened" to come to the field of a man named Boaz. Now, Boaz just "happened" to be a close relative of Naomi, who just "happened" to be a very wealthy man, who just "happened" to love Ruth at first sight, who just "happened" to be her kinsman redeemer.

Now, that's a whole lot of "just happenings." But I love how things "just happen" when the Lord is taking care of us and how He can turn things around one-hundred and eighty degrees for us. That's what He did for Ruth. And that's what He'll do for you when your situation requires it.

The death of Ruth's husband left her without a child and without a future. But when God blessed her with Boaz, her Kinsman-Redeemer, things turned around completely. Not only did Boaz provide her with the love of a caring husband and supplied all her material needs, God gave them a son, Obed, making her the great grandmother of King David and putting her in the blood line of Jesus, the Son of God. What a turnaround! Her life was never the same.

Child of God, don't give up when things seem hopeless. Jesus is your Kinsman-Redeemer. He's your close relative because He became a human-being like you. He's extremely wealthy, having ownership of heaven and earth, and everything in between. And like Boaz, He loved you at first sight and took you under His wings. You are the bride of Christ!

Lift up your head. Beautify yourself. Your story is still being written. Don't allow yourself to put a period where God has put comma. If Boaz could turn things around for Ruth so completely, can you imagine what Jesus, your heavenly Boaz, your kinsman-redeemer, will do for you?

Affirm Today:

"My story is still being written. I won't give up, I am resolute and I won't give in, I am tenacious. I am trusting You Lord to turn things around and finish my story in joy."

Additional Scriptures:

Ruth 4:14-17; Jeremiah 31:17; Genesis 26:13; Deuteronomy 29:9; Deuteronomy 8:18

Day 87

Hurry Up, God!

Phillips Brooks, a famous New England preacher, well-known for his calmness under pressure was one day feverishly pacing the floor. "What's the trouble, Phillips?" his friend asked. "The trouble," he responded, "is that I'm in a hurry, but God isn't!" I must confess I often feel that way too. And I won't be surprised if that is true for most people reading this devotional.

Now, because we are in a hurry and God seems to us to be taking His own time, one of our greatest temptations is to give up too soon. Spouses give up too soon on their marriages. Church members give up too soon on their church. Students give up too soon on their education. Businessmen too soon close shop. Artists too soon give up on their dream. "The tragedy with giving up too soon is that it ends the chance for God to work" (Lee McGlone).

As believers struggle with wayward children who are becoming more wayward, unfaithful spouses and unhappy homes, with sickness and death of friends and loved ones, financial needs, joblessness, feelings of rejection and persecution, with delayed answers to prayer, the danger is real that some may throw away their confidence, abandon their life of faith, and return to the world. While the danger is real that some could abandon their faith, what is certain is that He will never abandon them. While they may allow life to make them faithless, He will remain faithful to Himself and to them. When he says I will never leave you or forsake you, He means it.

That's why Scripture encourages us, not to cast away our confidence, but to imitate those who through faith and patience inherit the promises.

> *"For God is not unjust to forget your work and labor of love which you have shown toward His name, in that you have ministered to the saints, and do minister. And we desire that each one of you show the same diligence to the full assurance of hope until the end, that you do not become sluggish, but imitate those who through faith and patience inherit the promises. For when God made a promise to Abraham, because He could swear by no one greater, He swore by Himself, saying, 'Surely blessing I will bless you, and multiplying I will multiply you. And so, after he had patiently endured, he obtained the promise.'"*
> (Hebrews 6:10-15)

Abraham waited twenty-five years for Isaac to be born. In hope against hope, he continued to believe and grew strong in faith by continually giving glory to God, being fully persuaded He was able to perform what He had promised. Because Abraham was willing to cast his cares upon the Lord and exercise patience, he obtained the promise and is today, undoubtedly, one of the most revered men who ever lived, honored by Christians, Jews, and Muslims.

> *"So do not throw away your confidence; it will be richly rewarded. You need to persevere so that when you have done the will of God, you will receive what he has promised. For, "In just a little while, he who is coming will come and will not delay."* (Hebrews 10:35-37, NIV)

Child of God, I am realizing, more and more, faith does not work alone. Almost always, when it comes to obtaining promises, taking full delivery of our inheritance, and completing our assignment, our faith must be accompanied by patience. The good news, however, is that the patience you need, He supplies.

May the God of all patience strengthen you with His patience in your inner man and empower you by His Spirit to exercise patience and longsuffering with joy.

Affirm Today:

"I am resting as I wait with assurance for answered prayer. I am strengthened with His patience and empowered by His Spirit to exercise endurance joyfully."

Additional Scriptures:

Hebrews 6:10-15; Job 35:14; Hebrews 10:35-37; Romans 4:17; Ephesians 3:20

Day 88

Fight the Good Fight of Faith and Win

A re you fighting for your life, your health, your family?
How well are you doing? Are you winning? The only
fight I consider good is the one I win.

In 1 Timothy 6:12, Paul exhorts Timothy to *"fight the
good fight of faith."* Why? Because when we fight the fight
of faith we always win! Faith is the victory that overcomes
the world.

Listen to John's and Paul's exhortations to us:

> *"For whatever is born of God overcomes the
> world; and this is the victory that has over-
> come the world-our faith. Who is the one who
> overcomes the world, but he who believes
> that Jesus is the Son of God?"* (1 John
> 5:4-5, NASB)

> *"Fight the good fight of faith, lay hold on
> eternal life, whereunto thou art also called,
> and hast profession before many witnesses."*
> *(1 Timothy 6:12*, KJV)

We are not called to fight devils. We are not called to fight men. We are not called to fight circumstances, at least not directly. We are called to fight the good fight of faith. And when we do, God will cause us to live triumphantly in Christ Jesus. That means, He will cause us to experience the victory Jesus won for us personally in our current circumstances over all the works of our enemies.

Now, observe what the fight of faith focuses on. *"Lay hold of eternal life...,"* Paul says to Timothy. Literally, *"Keep taking hold of the eternal life to which you are called."* It does not focus on the enemy, or on the problem. It focuses on "the eternal life" within. The way to overcome all your adversaries is to use your faith to keep taking hold of "the eternal life" God mercifully gives to you in His Son.

Think of someone in danger of drowning. A lifeline is thrown out to him. It's within his reach. Now all he needs to do to be saved is to reach out and grab it. As soon as he grabs the lifeline, someone will pull him out of the water and out of danger. That's what eternal life is–God's lifeline that we grab hold of with our faith.

You were drowning in sin and satanic oppression of all kinds, and were helpless to deliver yourself. Then God sent you a lifeline. His name is Jesus. His life is "the eternal life" that overcomes the world, that destroys all the works of the enemy, and can deliver you out of all your afflictions. He is available to every man, but if you are already a child of God because you have received Jesus as your Savior, then the lifeline, "eternal life," is already inside of you. By using your faith to grab hold of it, it secures your victory!

Child of God, instead of focusing on your enemies, or on your problems, and trying to fight them directly, choose instead to focus your faith on the power and strength of "the eternal life" inside of you. Take hold of the "lifeline" that assures you victory by always focusing your mind on Christ as your life. And making bold confessions of His abilities with your mouth.

This means because you have "the eternal life" of God inside of you, you do not need to be worried or frightened in any way by the enemy. You just need to know and believe Jesus has already conquered them for you. Just keep meditating on the revelation that you have the indestructible, undefeatable, death-destroying, disease-healing, needs-supplying life of Jesus inside of you and keep boldly decreeing that all your enemies and troubles combined are not His equal. That's how you fight the good fight of faith and that's how you personally experience the victory that overcomes the world!

Affirm Today:

"Faith is the victory that overcomes the world. I have faith and I live in victory. I am focusing my mind and my choices on Jesus, the One Who overcomes the world. I refuse every problem and boldly decree that Jesus has conquered them all."

Additional Scriptures:

1 Timothy 6:12; 1 John 5:4-5; Ephesians 6:11-18; Deuteronomy 20:4; Exodus 15:3

Day 89

Supercharge Your Prayer Life

D o you want to pray with greater confidence? Would you like to exercise greater authority when you confront demonic powers? Are your doubts undermining your spiritual life and your prayers? Then you may need to supercharge your prayer life with fasting.

"Why could we not cast it out?" the disciples asked Jesus. *"Because of your unbelief,"* He responded. He attributed their prayer failure to unbelief. Unbelief is the greatest hindrance to answered prayer and the number one limiter of miracles in our lives. It needs to be resisted like the plague. Jesus proceeded to tell them how.

> *"For assuredly, I say to you, if you have faith as a mustard seed, you will say to this mountain, 'Move from here to there,' and it will move; and nothing will be impossible for you. However, this kind does not go out except by prayer and fasting."* (Matthew 17:19-20)

According to Jesus, they would have succeeded where they failed, if only they had given themselves to prayer and fasting. This means, if the disciples had given themselves to prayer and fasting, the unbelief that produced this prayer failure would have been overcome. And they would have obtained the breakthrough and received the miracle.

Now, this should be enough of a reason for every disciple of Christ to include fasting as a spiritual discipline. Clearly, it is an effective means of overcoming unbelief and strengthening faith. It supercharges our prayer life, allowing us to obtain results we would not have otherwise.

Why is fasting so powerful? It does not change God–God does not need changing! He already loves us as much as He loves Jesus and is more than able to answer any prayer we pray. And it does not change circumstances–God does that in response to prayer. The power of fasting is the effects it has on us.

I find that when I choose to fast for several days, it weakens the influence of my physical senses on my mind and it strengthens the influence of my spiritual senses on my perception. It makes me more conscious of things I cannot see and more able to perceive the presence and activity of the Spirit. This heightened spiritual sensitivity overcomes unbelief and reinforces my faith. The result is that I speak with greater authority and confidence, and am able to release the anointing that abides in me in a greater way. This anointing breaks yokes and produces powerful answers to prayer.

Another reason fasting is so effective is that it is a potent expression of humility. When you choose to go without food for a period of time to focus on God and give yourself to prayer, you are admitting that you are totally dependent upon Him and that the answer you need is not found in you. You are casting yourself upon Him fully and looking to Him only. This act of extreme humility triggers the flow of grace resulting in outstanding answers to prayer.

> *"But He gives more grace." Therefore He says: 'God resists the proud, But gives grace to the humble.' Therefore submit to God. Resist the devil and he will flee from you...Humble yourselves in the sight of the Lord, and He will lift you up."* (James 4:6-7, 10)

Child of God, you do not have to fast. It is not a law you must obey to obtain favor with God. Jesus did that for you. But you may need to fast to resist successfully the unbelief that is hindering your prayers and keeping you from walking in His favor. You may need to fast to increase your sensitivity to the things of the Spirit. You may need to fast as a way of humbling yourself and triggering the flow of grace God gives to the humble. And when you do, your prayer life will go to another level. It will be supercharged. And prayer failures will become prayer victories!

Affirm Today:

"I am ready to take my prayer life to another level and embrace this change wholeheartedly. Lord I accept Your abundant grace and ask that You guide me. Meet me in prayer and lift me up."

Additional Scriptures:

Matthew 17:19-20; James 4:6-7, 10; Luke 11:2; Luke 18:1; Romans 8:26

Day 90

You Won!

Feeling discouraged? Think you've been defeated? Seems the enemy has the upper hand? Discouragement is a common emotion. But for the child of God, it is always the result of incomplete information. A small misunderstanding can generate unnecessary anxiety.

When the Battle of Waterloo was fought two-hundred years ago, the British waited with baited breath for the outcome. Finally, using the method of communication available to them before the age of the telephone and internet, the message began to appear in the sky, being spelled out one letter at a time. "Wellington defeated ...." Those two words could be seen clearly. Then a thick fog filled the air. Not being able to see any other words, the people thought they'd lost. Understandably, gloom and discouragement set in. That's because they thought this was the end of the message. But it wasn't! After a while, another two words came through: "Wellington defeated...the enemy." And discouragement gave way to joy!

The fog of life is real, and sometimes, it's thick enough to hide God's love and power from your eyes. But while the fog may make it difficult for you to see, the fog cannot change the truth. Jesus defeated the enemy. And, in the end, you win!

Here is the complete message:

> *"These things I have spoken to you, that in Me you may have peace. In the world you will have tribulation; but be of good cheer, I have overcome the world."* (John 16:33)

> *"Now may the God of peace Himself sanctify you completely; and may your whole spirit, soul, and body be preserved blameless at the coming of our Lord Jesus Christ. He who calls you is faithful, who also will do it."* (1 Thessalonians 5:23-24)

Child of God, don't allow the fog to deprive you of joy. Read the entire message. Believe God's report. "Jesus defeated...the enemy." You won!

Affirm Today:

"I believe God's report. Jesus defeated the enemy and I win!"

Additional Scriptures:

John 16:3; I Thessalonians 5:23-24; 1 John 5:4; Luke 10:19; Revelation 12:11

God bless you! If this book has helped you please let
us know.

Bethel World Outreach Church - City of Hope
16227 Batchellors Forest Road
Olney, MD 20832
Tel. 301-588-8099; Fax. 301-774-1940

Also by Bishop Johnson
*Light for Your Journey: Essential Building Blocks for a
Successful Life*
Anointed for the Marketplace
This One Thing I Do
Good-bye Worry
"A Moment of Grace," Blog and TV Program

Connect With Us!

www.darlingstonjohnson.org
Web: bethelcityofhope.com
Email: info@bwomi.org
F /bethelcityofhope
T @bwoccityofhope
YouTube: bwoccityofhope